UNRAVELLING THE WEALTH PARADOX: NAVIGATING SUCCESS BEYOND DEGREES

Elham Oustan

ISBN:9798883911070

Cover design by: Art Painter
Library of Congress Control Number: 2018675309
Printed in the United States of America

CONTENTS

INTRODUCTION

The common narrative dictates that the path to wealth and success lies in the corridors of academia, where degrees and certificates pave the way to prosperity. Yet, the reality often defies this conventional wisdom. It's a truth seldom acknowledged: the pursuit of higher education or the acquisition of new skills does not guarantee riches. In fact, if we examine the landscape of millionaires, we find a striking absence of formal education among many of them. They haven't amassed wealth through prestigious degrees or academic accolades. Instead, they've mastered the art of making money.

This revelation challenges the traditional notions ingrained in society. We've been led to believe that success is synonymous with academic achievements, that the key to financial abundance lies in the pursuit of higher education. But the truth is far more nuanced. While education undoubtedly holds value, it alone does not pave the road to prosperity. The real secret to wealth lies in understanding the mechanisms of wealth creation, in learning the ins and outs of financial independence.

One of the most perplexing truths is that those who have achieved financial success often benefit from the misguided pursuits of others. They capitalize on the societal pressure to pursue higher education, enticing us to invest our time and resources in academic endeavors that may not necessarily lead to financial freedom. In doing so, they perpetuate a cycle wherein the masses remain ensnared in the pursuit of credentials, while the truly affluent focus on strategies for wealth accumulation.

So why do we find ourselves trapped in this cycle of chasing degrees and certifications? Perhaps it's because we've been conditioned to believe that education is the great equalizer, the pathway to a better life. And while education undoubtedly opens doors, it's imperative to recognize its limitations. We must acknowledge that the ability to make money transcends the confines of formal education. It's a skill that can be learned and honed, regardless of one's academic background.

In the pages that follow, we'll delve into the untold truths of wealth creation. We'll explore the strategies employed by self-made millionaires, uncovering the secrets they don't teach in classrooms. From leveraging opportunities to mastering the art of negotiation, we'll dissect the fundamental principles that underpin financial success. It's time to shatter the illusions that bind us and embark on a journey towards true prosperity— a journey rooted not in degrees, but in the pursuit of financial literacy and entrepreneurial acumen.

CHAPTER 1: BEYOND THE DICHOTOMY: RETHINKING SUCCESS IN A CHANGING WORLD

Section 1: Introduction to societal perceptions of success tied to economic privilege and academic achievement

In this section, we delve deeply into the societal perceptions that tightly tether success to economic privilege and academic achievement. We explore how these perceptions are deeply ingrained within cultural norms and how they shape individual aspirations and societal values.

1. Cultural Conditioning and Social Norms:

Cultural conditioning and social norms play a pivotal role in shaping our perceptions of success. From an early age, individuals are inundated with messages that reinforce the association between success and material wealth, leading to a deeply ingrained belief that economic prosperity is the ultimate measure of achievement.

Media Influence:

One of the primary vehicles through which this narrative is perpetuated is the media. Television shows, movies, advertisements, and social media platforms bombard audiences with images of opulent lifestyles, showcasing affluent individuals living in luxurious homes, driving expensive cars, and wearing designer clothes. These portrayals create an aspirational ideal that suggests material possessions are synonymous with success and happiness. Furthermore, success stories in the media often focus on individuals who have amassed vast fortunes through entrepreneurship, investment, or inheritance, further reinforcing the notion that financial wealth is the pinnacle of achievement.

Social Comparison:

In addition to media influence, social dynamics within communities and peer groups also contribute to the cultivation of these beliefs. Social comparison theory suggests that individuals evaluate their own worth based on comparisons with others, particularly those within their social circle. In a culture that glorifies materialism and wealth, individuals may feel pressure to keep up with the perceived successes of their peers, leading to a cycle of conspicuous consumption and status-seeking behaviors. This phenomenon is particularly pronounced in affluent communities, where there is often intense competition to display wealth and social status through conspicuous consumption.

Educational System:

The educational system also plays a role in reinforcing societal perceptions of success. Academic institutions often prioritize standardized testing, grades, and prestigious university admissions as measures of achievement. Students are encouraged to excel academically in pursuit of lucrative career opportunities and societal recognition. However, this narrow focus on academic success overlooks other forms of intelligence and personal growth, perpetuating the belief that success is synonymous with intellectual achievement.

Cultural Values and Traditions:

Cultural values and traditions also contribute to the construction of success narratives. In some cultures, financial success is equated with social status and respectability, leading individuals to prioritize wealth accumulation as a means of fulfilling societal expectations. Additionally, cultural norms surrounding family, community, and social obligations may influence individuals' perceptions of success, shaping their aspirations and priorities.

Impact on Identity and Self-Worth:

The pervasive influence of these cultural narratives can have profound effects on individuals' sense of identity and self-worth. Those who fall short of societal expectations may experience feelings of inadequacy, shame, and worthlessness, leading to psychological distress and diminished well-being. Conversely, those who achieve conventional markers of success may experience pressure to maintain their status and fear of failure or loss.

In summary, cultural conditioning and social norms create a powerful framework through which success is defined and perceived. By understanding the mechanisms through which these narratives are constructed and perpetuated, we can begin to challenge their influence and cultivate a more inclusive and holistic understanding of success.

The Myth of the Meritocracy:

"The Myth of the Meritocracy" is a concept that challenges the widely-held belief that success is solely determined by individual talent and effort. It suggests that in a truly meritocratic society, everyone would have an equal opportunity to succeed based on their abilities and hard work. However, upon closer examination, it becomes evident that various structural barriers and inequalities exist, undermining the notion of a level playing field.

Structural Barriers and Inequalities:

One of the key factors that undermines the meritocratic ideal is the presence of structural barriers and systemic inequalities. These barriers can take many forms, including socioeconomic status, race, gender, and access to resources. Economic privilege, in particular, plays a significant role in shaping opportunities for success. Individuals born into affluent families often have access to resources such as inherited wealth, private education, and social connections that provide them with a head start in life. Conversely, those born into poverty or marginalized communities face significant obstacles in accessing the same opportunities, perpetuating cycles of disadvantage.

Inherited Wealth and Social Capital:

Inherited wealth is a prime example of how economic privilege can perpetuate inequality across generations. Individuals born into wealthy families inherit not only financial resources but also social capital—the networks, connections, and cultural knowledge that provide access to opportunities and influence. This inherited advantage gives them a significant leg up in areas such as education, employment, and entrepreneurship, further widening the gap between the haves and the have-nots. Similarly, individuals from marginalized backgrounds may lack access to these resources, limiting their ability to compete on an equal footing.

Access to Quality Education:

Access to quality education is another critical determinant of success that is often unequally distributed. While education is often touted as the great equalizer, the reality is that disparities in funding, resources, and educational attainment exist across different communities. Schools in affluent neighborhoods tend to receive more funding and resources, resulting in better facilities, smaller class sizes, and more experienced teachers. In contrast, schools in low-income areas often struggle with overcrowded classrooms, outdated resources, and limited extracurricular opportunities. These disparities can have a profound impact on students' academic outcomes and future prospects, perpetuating cycles of poverty and inequality.

Critical Reflection on Success:
By highlighting these disparities, we aim to challenge the myth of the meritocracy and encourage critical reflection on the roots of success. Success is not solely determined by individual talent and effort but is influenced by a complex interplay of factors, including structural barriers, systemic inequalities, and inherited advantages. By acknowledging these realities, we can begin to address the root causes of inequality and work towards creating a more equitable society where everyone has the opportunity to thrive based on their abilities and potential, rather than their socioeconomic background.

Academic Achievement as a Proxy for Success:
"Academic Achievement as a Proxy for Success" delves into the pervasive notion in many societies that academic success is synonymous with overall success. We examine how the pursuit of higher education has been elevated as the primary pathway to upward mobility, with degrees and academic credentials often serving as the ultimate markers of intelligence, competence, and societal worth.

Cultural Perception of Academic Achievement:
We begin by exploring the cultural norms and societal expectations that equate academic achievement with success. From an early age, children are taught that excelling in school is crucial for future success. Parents, teachers, and peers often emphasize the importance of obtaining good grades, gaining admission to prestigious universities, and securing high-paying jobs. This cultural emphasis on academic success reinforces the belief that educational attainment is the key to unlocking opportunities and achieving social mobility.

Reinforcement of Power Structures:

However, we challenge the assumption that academic success is a true reflection of one's potential or abilities. Instead, we argue that the emphasis on academic achievement often serves to reinforce existing power structures and privilege. Individuals from privileged backgrounds, who have access to resources such as private tutors, enrichment programs, and educational opportunities, are more likely to excel academically and gain admission to elite institutions. This perpetuates a cycle of advantage, where those who are already privileged are further advantaged by the educational system.

Marginalization of Non-traditional Paths:

Furthermore, we discuss how the emphasis on academic achievement can marginalize individuals who do not conform to traditional educational norms or who pursue alternative pathways to success. Not everyone thrives in a traditional classroom setting, and individuals with diverse talents, interests, and learning styles may struggle to excel academically. Additionally, socioeconomic barriers, such as poverty, lack of access to quality education, and systemic inequalities, can further hinder academic success for marginalized communities. As a result, individuals who do not fit the mold of academic success may be unfairly stigmatized or overlooked, perpetuating cycles of marginalization and exclusion.

Call for a Holistic Definition of Success:

In light of these challenges, we advocate for a more holistic definition of success that goes beyond academic achievement. Success should be measured not only by educational credentials but also by qualities such as creativity, resilience, adaptability, and real-world experience. We celebrate individuals who forge their own paths to success, whether through entrepreneurship, vocational training, creative pursuits, or community engagement. By broadening our understanding of success, we can create a more inclusive society that recognizes and values diverse forms of achievement, regardless of academic pedigree or socioeconomic background.

4. Social Validation and Conformity:

"Social Validation and Conformity" explores the powerful influence of societal norms and expectations on individuals' perceptions of success and self-worth. We delve into how society's reinforcement of certain measures of success, particularly those tied to economic privilege, creates a culture of conformity and external validation.

Pressure to Conform to Societal Expectations:

We begin by examining how society defines and values success, often equating it with material wealth, prestigious job titles, and social status. From an early age, individuals are socialized to aspire to these conventional markers of success, as they are celebrated and rewarded by society. This societal pressure to conform to established norms creates a powerful incentive for individuals to prioritize external validation over personal fulfillment. As a result, many individuals feel compelled to pursue paths that align with societal expectations, even if it means sacrificing their own dreams and authenticity.

Reinforcement of Economic Privilege:

Furthermore, we explore how societal validation perpetuates the link between success and economic privilege. Society often confers status and respect upon those who have achieved financial success, reinforcing the belief that wealth and status are indicators of personal worth and achievement. This reinforcement of economic privilege not only perpetuates existing inequalities but also creates a culture of competition and comparison, where individuals constantly measure their success against others based on material possessions and social status.

Sacrifice of Authenticity for Approval:

In the pursuit of social validation, individuals may find themselves sacrificing their authenticity and values to conform to societal expectations. They may choose career paths, lifestyles, or relationships based on external measures of success rather than their own passions and aspirations. This can lead to feelings of emptiness, disconnection, and lack of fulfillment, as individuals prioritize the approval of others over their own well-being and happiness.

Impact on Mental Health and Well-being:

The pressure to conform to societal expectations and seek external validation can take a toll on individuals' mental health and well-being. Constantly striving to meet unrealistic standards of success can lead to stress, anxiety, depression, and burnout. Additionally, the fear of judgment and rejection can prevent individuals from pursuing their true passions and expressing their authentic selves, leading to feelings of alienation and dissatisfaction.

Promoting Authenticity and Self-Validation:

In light of these challenges, we advocate for a shift towards promoting authenticity and self-validation as measures of success. Rather than seeking approval from others, individuals should be encouraged to define success on their own terms and prioritize their own values, passions, and well-being. This requires challenging societal norms and expectations, fostering a culture of acceptance and inclusivity, and celebrating diverse forms of achievement beyond material wealth and status. By promoting authenticity and self-validation, we can create a more compassionate and supportive society where individuals are empowered to pursue paths that align with their true selves and lead to genuine fulfillment.

5. Impact on Mental Health and Well-being:

The section "Impact on Mental Health and Well-being" delves into the profound psychological consequences of living in a society where success is narrowly defined and often inaccessible to many individuals. We examine how the relentless pursuit of conventional markers of success, such as economic prosperity and academic achievement, can have detrimental effects on mental health and overall well-being.

Feelings of Inadequacy and Self-doubt:
One of the primary impacts of societal pressure to achieve narrow definitions of success is the pervasive sense of inadequacy and self-doubt that many individuals experience. Constantly comparing oneself to societal standards of success can lead to feelings of inadequacy, as individuals may perceive themselves as falling short of unrealistic expectations. This can erode self-esteem and confidence, fueling a cycle of self-doubt and negative self-talk.

Anxiety and Stress:
The relentless pursuit of economic success and academic achievement can also contribute to heightened levels of anxiety and stress. Individuals may feel overwhelmed by the pressure to excel in their careers, meet societal expectations, and achieve financial stability. This chronic stress can manifest in physical symptoms such as headaches, insomnia, and fatigue, as well as psychological symptoms such as racing thoughts, irritability, and difficulty concentrating.

Depression and Burnout:
In some cases, the pressure to conform to societal norms of success can lead to depression and burnout. The constant striving for external validation and the fear of failure can take a significant toll on mental health, leading to feelings of hopelessness, despair, and emotional exhaustion. Individuals may lose interest in activities they once enjoyed, withdraw from social interactions, and experience a sense of emptiness or numbness.

Social Isolation and Alienation:

Furthermore, the emphasis on individual achievement and competition can contribute to feelings of social isolation and alienation. In a society where success is narrowly defined and individuals are pitted against one another in a race for success, genuine connections and relationships may suffer. Individuals may feel disconnected from others, as they struggle to maintain appearances and compete for limited resources and opportunities.

Importance of Redefining Success:

In light of these challenges, we emphasize the importance of challenging societal norms and redefining success in ways that prioritize holistic well-being and fulfillment. Success should not be measured solely by external markers such as wealth, status, and academic credentials, but by factors such as personal growth, resilience, and overall life satisfaction. By shifting the focus from external validation to internal fulfillment, individuals can cultivate a greater sense of purpose, meaning, and well-being in their lives. This requires challenging societal pressures, fostering a culture of acceptance and inclusivity, and supporting individuals in pursuing paths that align with their values and aspirations. Ultimately, by redefining success in more holistic terms, we can create a society that values the well-being and flourishing of all its members.

By dissecting the societal perceptions of success tied to economic privilege and academic achievement, we aim to lay the groundwork for a more nuanced understanding of success—one that celebrates diversity, resilience, and authenticity.

Section 2: Personal anecdotes challenging these perceptions and highlighting the multifaceted nature of success

From my earliest memories, a pervasive belief permeated the fabric of our society, whispering its influence into the ears of children and adults alike: your destiny is predetermined by the size of your father's wallet. Those fortunate enough to be born into wealth were often assured that the pursuit of academic excellence was optional, even unnecessary. After all, why invest time and effort in education when financial prosperity was seemingly guaranteed? Conversely, for those from more modest backgrounds, the narrative was starkly different. We were told that the key to success lay in our ability to outwork and outlearn our circumstances, that our future hinged upon our capacity to accumulate degrees and skills like pieces on a chessboard.

Yet, as the tapestry of my life began to unfold, I found myself encountering threads of contradiction woven into the fabric of this societal narrative. The future, it appeared, had a penchant for defying expectations. It became increasingly evident to me that success was not merely a binary equation dictated by economic privilege or academic prowess. Rather, it was a multifaceted tapestry, intricately woven with threads of ambition, resilience, adaptability, and the seizing of fleeting opportunities.

My journey thus far has been a testament to the transformative power of challenging prevailing ideologies and embracing the complexity of human experience. It is a story of breaking free from the shackles of predetermined destinies, of navigating the labyrinth of societal expectations, and ultimately, of forging a path uniquely my own.

In the forthcoming chapters, I invite you to embark on a journey alongside me—an exploration of the twists and turns, triumphs and tribulations that have shaped my understanding of success. Through the prism of my experiences, I aim to illuminate the diverse pathways to fulfillment and achievement that transcend the narrow dichotomy of wealth versus education. For in the kaleidoscope of life, success reveals itself in myriad forms, awaiting those bold enough to challenge convention and embrace the boundless possibilities that lie beyond the confines of societal expectation.

Section 3: Exploration of the complexities of success

In this section, we delve into the multifaceted nature of

success, examining the various qualities and attributes that contribute to achievement and fulfillment. We explore the complexities of success through the lens of ambition, resilience, adaptability, and seizing opportunities, recognizing that these qualities are essential for navigating the challenges and uncertainties of life.

Ambition:

Ambition is the driving force behind many individuals' pursuit of success. It encompasses the desire to set and achieve goals, to strive for excellence, and to fulfill one's potential. However, ambition is not solely about climbing the corporate ladder or accumulating wealth; it can also manifest in personal growth, creative expression, and social impact. By exploring the diverse manifestations of ambition, we highlight the importance of setting meaningful goals and pursuing them with passion and determination.

Resilience:

Resilience is the ability to bounce back from setbacks, overcome adversity, and thrive in the face of challenges. It involves cultivating inner strength, perseverance, and a positive mindset, even in the midst of difficult circumstances. Resilience is crucial for success because it allows individuals to weather the inevitable ups and downs of life without losing sight of their goals or giving in to despair. By exploring stories of resilience, we underscore the importance of perseverance and tenacity in achieving long-term success.

Adaptability:

Adaptability is the capacity to adjust to change, to embrace new opportunities, and to learn and grow from experience. In today's rapidly changing world, adaptability is a critical skill for success, enabling individuals to thrive in dynamic environments and navigate uncertainty with confidence. Whether it's pivoting to a new career path, embracing emerging technologies, or responding to shifting market trends, adaptability allows individuals to remain agile and resilient in the face of change.

Seizing Opportunities:

Success often involves recognizing and seizing opportunities for growth, innovation, and advancement. This requires a combination of vision, strategic thinking, and decisive action. By exploring stories of individuals who have capitalized on opportunities, we highlight the importance of being proactive, resourceful, and open-minded in pursuing success. Whether it's taking calculated risks, networking with influential contacts, or leveraging one's skills and talents, seizing opportunities is essential for realizing one's full potential and achieving long-term success.

Conclusion:

In conclusion, the exploration of the complexities of success reveals that achievement and fulfillment are multifaceted concepts that encompass a range of qualities and attributes. By embracing ambition, resilience, adaptability, and the ability to seize opportunities, individuals can navigate the complexities of life with confidence and purpose, realizing their dreams and making a meaningful impact on the world. Ultimately, success is not defined by external measures alone but by the journey of growth, self-discovery, and contribution that leads to a fulfilling and purposeful life.

Section 4: Invitation to readers to embark on a journey of self-discovery and exploration of diverse pathways to fulfillment

In this section, we extend an invitation to readers to embark on a journey of self-discovery and exploration of diverse pathways to fulfillment. We encourage readers to engage with the content presented in the book as a catalyst for personal growth, reflection, and transformation.

Embracing Personal Exploration:

We invite readers to approach the content with an open mind and a willingness to explore new perspectives and possibilities. By embracing curiosity and self-exploration, readers can uncover insights about their own values, passions, and aspirations, leading to a deeper understanding of what success means to them on a personal level.

Reflecting on Individual Goals and Values:

We encourage readers to take time to reflect on their individual goals, values, and priorities in life. What brings them joy and fulfillment? What are their long-term aspirations and dreams? By engaging in introspection and self-reflection, readers can gain clarity about their personal definition of success and the paths they want to pursue to achieve it.

Exploring Diverse Pathways to Fulfillment:

Readers are invited to explore the diverse pathways to fulfillment presented in the book, recognizing that there is no one-size-fits-all approach to success. Through personal anecdotes, case studies, and insights shared in the book, readers can gain inspiration and perspective on the myriad ways in which individuals have found meaning and purpose in their lives.

Challenging Societal Norms and Expectations:

We encourage readers to challenge societal norms and expectations surrounding success, recognizing that these standards may not align with their own values and aspirations. By questioning conventional measures of success and embracing alternative definitions of fulfillment, readers can liberate themselves from the pressure to conform and chart their own unique paths to happiness and well-being.

Taking Action and Pursuing Growth:

Finally, we invite readers to take action on their journey of self-discovery and exploration. This may involve setting goals, pursuing new opportunities, seeking out mentors and role models, and engaging in personal development activities. By taking proactive steps towards personal growth and fulfillment, readers can create meaningful and fulfilling lives that are aligned with their true selves.

Conclusion:

In conclusion, the invitation to readers to embark on a journey of self-discovery and exploration is a call to action to engage with the content presented in the book as a catalyst for personal transformation. By embracing curiosity, reflection, and action, readers can uncover their own pathways to fulfillment and create lives that are authentic, meaningful, and aligned with their deepest values and aspirations.

CHAPTER 2: "THE ILLUSION OF PREPAREDNESS: A JOURNEY BEYOND EXPECTATIONS"

Section 1: Personal narrative of relentless pursuit of academic excellence and skill acquisition

From the earliest moments of my childhood, I exhibited an insatiable curiosity that knew no bounds. I approached learning with an enthusiasm that bordered on obsession, eagerly devouring any book or resource that promised to expand my understanding of the world. My parents often found me tucked away in a corner, engrossed in the pages of an encyclopedia or lost in the intricate patterns of a foreign language workbook. As I grew older, this thirst for knowledge only intensified, propelling me towards a path of academic excellence and skill acquisition.

In school, I was known as the student who never settled for mediocrity. While my peers were content with surface-level understanding, I sought to delve deeper, to unravel the mysteries that lay beneath the surface. I spent countless hours poring over textbooks, immersing myself in subjects ranging from mathematics to history to literature. But my hunger for knowledge extended far beyond the confines of the classroom. I sought out extracurricular activities that allowed me to explore new interests and develop practical skills. Whether it was learning to knit from my grandmother or attending weekend workshops on computer programming, I seized every opportunity to expand my horizons and broaden my skill set.

This relentless pursuit of academic excellence and skill acquisition became the driving force behind everything I did. I approached each challenge with unwavering determination, refusing to be deterred by obstacles or setbacks. And with each new milestone I achieved—whether it was earning top marks on an exam or mastering a new language—I felt a sense of exhilaration that only fueled my desire to continue pushing myself further. In my quest for excellence, there was no such thing as complacency. There was only the relentless pursuit of knowledge, the ceaseless striving towards a higher standard of achievement.

Section 2: Reflection on the realization that extensive qualifications and experience may not adequately prepare for challenges

For years, I operated under the assumption that success was synonymous with hard work and dedication. I believed that if I could just accumulate enough qualifications and experience, I would be impervious to the challenges that lay ahead. But as I ventured out into the real world, I quickly discovered that this belief was nothing more than an illusion.

The world outside the hallowed halls of academia was far more complex and unpredictable than I had ever imagined. No amount of degrees or accolades could shield me from the harsh realities of life—the uncertainty, the ambiguity, the ever-present possibility of failure. It was a sobering realization, one that forced me to confront the limitations of my own ambition and the fallibility of my assumptions.

I soon found myself facing challenges that no amount of

preparation could have adequately prepared me for. Whether it was navigating the intricacies of interpersonal relationships in the workplace or grappling with the unpredictable nature of the global economy, I found myself struggling to adapt to a world that seemed determined to thwart my carefully laid plans. It was a humbling experience—one that shattered my confidence and left me questioning everything I thought I knew about success and achievement.

Section 3: Humbling experiences and setbacks leading to self-discovery and growth

In the wake of these unexpected challenges, I found myself at a crossroads. I could either succumb to defeat and retreat back into the safety of my comfort zone, or I could embrace adversity as an opportunity for growth and self-discovery. I chose the latter.

Each setback became a lesson in resilience, teaching me to pick myself up and dust myself off in the face of failure. I learned to view adversity not as a roadblock, but as a stepping stone on the path to personal growth and development. With each new challenge I faced, I discovered new strengths and abilities within myself—resilience in the face of uncertainty, adaptability in the midst of chaos, and perseverance in the face of adversity.

It was a transformative process—one that pushed me to confront my deepest fears and insecurities, and emerge stronger on the other side. I came to understand that true growth only comes from stepping outside of one's comfort zone, from embracing the unknown and facing it head-on. And though the journey was fraught with obstacles and setbacks, it was also filled with moments of triumph and self-discovery—moments that reminded me of the boundless potential that lies within each and every one of us.

Section 4: Emphasis on the importance of adaptability and resilience in the face of uncertainty

Armed with the wisdom gleaned from my experiences, I

embarked on a new journey—one guided not by rigid plans and unwavering certainty, but by a willingness to embrace uncertainty and adaptability. I came to understand that true success is not measured solely by academic accolades or professional achievements, but by the ability to navigate life's uncertainties with grace and resilience.

In a world that is constantly changing and evolving, adaptability is the key to survival. It is through our failures that we discover the boundless potential of the human spirit, and it is through adversity that true resilience is forged. By embracing change and uncertainty, we open ourselves up to new possibilities and opportunities for growth. And though the road ahead may be fraught with challenges, I am confident that with the right mindset and the right attitude, we can overcome anything that stands in our way.

CHAPTER 3: "THE POWER OF MINDSET: CULTIVATING A WEALTH MENTALITY"

Section 1: Exploration of the impact of mindset on financial outcomes

Understanding the intricate connection between mindset and financial outcomes is crucial for anyone seeking to build wealth and financial stability. This section delves into the profound influence of mindset on financial success, drawing upon psychological theories and research findings to illuminate the mechanisms at play.

Psychological Theories:

1. Fixed vs. Growth Mindset:

One of the seminal theories regarding mindset comes from the work of psychologist Carol Dweck, who introduced the concepts of fixed and growth mindsets. Individuals with a fixed mindset believe that their abilities and intelligence are static traits, leading them to avoid challenges and view failures as reflections of their inherent shortcomings. In contrast, those with a growth mindset perceive abilities as malleable through effort and learning, embracing challenges and persisting in the face of setbacks.

Applied to financial matters, individuals with a growth mindset are more likely to view setbacks such as financial losses or setbacks as temporary hurdles to overcome through learning and adaptation. They are more inclined to seek out opportunities for improvement and view financial success as achievable through effort and perseverance.

2. Scarcity Mentality vs. Abundance Mentality:

Psychologist Stephen Covey introduced the concepts of scarcity and abundance mentalities in his book "The 7 Habits of Highly Effective People." Those with a scarcity mentality perceive resources as limited, leading to a fear of scarcity and a competitive mindset. In contrast, individuals with an abundance mentality believe in the abundance of opportunities and resources, leading to a mindset of collaboration and generosity.

When applied to finances, those with a scarcity mentality may hoard wealth, fear taking risks, and engage in zero-sum thinking, viewing others' successes as threats to their own. On the other hand, individuals with an abundance mentality are more likely to invest in opportunities, share knowledge and resources, and approach financial decisions with optimism and openness.

Research Findings:

Numerous studies have provided empirical evidence of the profound impact of mindset on financial outcomes:

1. Behavioral Economics:

Research in behavioral economics has demonstrated how cognitive biases and irrational decision-making patterns can lead to suboptimal financial choices. For example, the framing effect shows how the presentation of information can significantly influence decision-making, leading individuals to make different choices based on how options are presented.

2. Neuroeconomics:

Neuroeconomics explores the neural mechanisms underlying economic decision-making. Studies using techniques such as fMRI scans have revealed how emotions, cognitive processes, and social influences interact to shape financial behaviors. For instance, researchers have identified brain regions associated with risk aversion, loss aversion, and reward anticipation, shedding light on the neural basis of financial decision-making.

3. Positive Psychology:

Positive psychology emphasizes the role of positive emotions, strengths, and virtues in promoting well-being and resilience. Studies have shown how factors such as gratitude, optimism, and resilience can influence financial outcomes by shaping individuals' attitudes towards money, risk-taking behavior, and ability to bounce back from setbacks.

In summary, the impact of mindset on financial outcomes is profound and multifaceted, encompassing cognitive, emotional, and social dimensions. By understanding the psychological theories and empirical findings underlying mindset, individuals can cultivate a wealth mentality and unlock their potential for financial success.

Section 2: Examination of specific mindset shifts necessary for building wealth

Building wealth isn't just about making money; it's about cultivating the right mindset that enables financial success. In this section, we'll delve into the specific mindset shifts necessary for building wealth, including embracing abundance, resilience in the face of setbacks, and a willingness to take calculated risks.

Embracing Abundance:

Embracing abundance means viewing the world as a place of limitless opportunities rather than scarcity. Those with an abundance mindset believe that there's more than enough wealth, resources, and success to go around. Instead of feeling threatened by the success of others, they celebrate it, knowing that there's plenty of room for everyone to thrive.

Cultivating an abundance mindset involves shifting your focus from what you lack to what you have and what you can create. This mindset encourages gratitude, optimism, and a proactive approach to life. Rather than dwelling on limitations, individuals with an abundance mindset seek out opportunities, collaborate with others, and remain open to new possibilities.

Resilience in the Face of Setbacks:

Building wealth is rarely a linear journey; it's filled with ups and downs, challenges, and setbacks. What sets successful wealth builders apart is their ability to bounce back from adversity with resilience. Resilience is the capacity to recover quickly from difficulties, setbacks, and failures, and to adapt and grow stronger as a result.

Resilient individuals understand that setbacks are not permanent roadblocks but temporary hurdles to overcome. They maintain a positive outlook, learn from their failures, and use setbacks as opportunities for growth and development. Rather than being discouraged by obstacles, they become more determined and resourceful, finding alternative paths to achieve their goals.

A Willingness to Take Calculated Risks:

Building wealth often requires stepping outside of your comfort zone and taking calculated risks. However, these risks shouldn't be reckless; they should be carefully considered and based on thorough research and analysis. Successful wealth builders understand that calculated risks are essential for growth and innovation.

Taking calculated risks involves weighing the potential rewards against the potential downsides and making informed decisions accordingly. It requires courage, confidence, and a willingness to embrace uncertainty. While not every risk will pay off, those who are willing to take calculated risks are more likely to seize opportunities and achieve greater financial success in the long run.

In conclusion, cultivating the right mindset is crucial for building wealth. By embracing abundance, resilience, and a willingness to take calculated risks, individuals can overcome obstacles, seize opportunities, and ultimately achieve their financial goals. These mindset shifts not only impact financial outcomes but also lead to greater fulfillment and success in all areas of life.

Section 3: Practical exercises and strategies for developing and maintaining a wealth mindset

Developing and maintaining a wealth mindset requires consistent effort and practice. In this section, we'll explore practical exercises and strategies that can help individuals cultivate the right mindset for building wealth. These exercises encompass visualization techniques, affirmations, and gratitude practices, all designed to rewire the way we think about money and success.

Visualization Techniques:

Visualization is a powerful tool for programming the subconscious mind and aligning our thoughts and actions with our financial goals. By vividly imagining ourselves achieving success and experiencing abundance, we can create a mental blueprint for the life we desire.

To practice visualization, find a quiet and comfortable space where you won't be disturbed. Close your eyes and envision your ideal financial future in detail. Picture yourself achieving your financial goals, whether it's buying a dream home, starting a successful business, or traveling the world. Engage all your senses to make the visualization as vivid and realistic as possible.

Regular practice of visualization can help reinforce positive beliefs about money and success, increase motivation and confidence, and attract opportunities that align with your vision.

Affirmations:
Affirmations are positive statements that affirm the reality we want to create in our lives. By repeating affirmations regularly, we can reprogram our subconscious mind and overcome limiting beliefs about money and wealth.

Create a list of affirmations that reflect your financial goals and aspirations. For example, "I am worthy of abundance and success," "Money flows to me effortlessly and abundantly," or "I am grateful for the wealth and abundance in my life." Repeat these affirmations aloud or in your mind several times a day, ideally in the morning and before bed.

Consistent practice of affirmations can help shift your mindset from scarcity to abundance, boost self-confidence, and attract positive experiences and opportunities that support your financial goals.

Gratitude Practices:
Gratitude is a powerful antidote to feelings of scarcity and lack. By focusing on what we're grateful for, we shift our attention away from what we lack and cultivate a mindset of abundance and appreciation.

Incorporate gratitude practices into your daily routine by keeping a gratitude journal. Each day, write down three things you're grateful for, including both big and small blessings in your life. Take time to reflect on the abundance that surrounds you, whether it's supportive relationships, good health, or moments of joy and fulfillment.

Practicing gratitude regularly can help rewire your brain for positivity, reduce stress and anxiety, and foster a greater sense of well-being and contentment.

In conclusion, developing and maintaining a wealth mindset requires consistent practice and commitment. By incorporating visualization techniques, affirmations, and gratitude practices into your daily routine, you can reprogram your subconscious mind, overcome limiting beliefs, and align your thoughts and actions with your financial goals. These practical exercises empower you to cultivate a mindset of abundance, resilience, and prosperity, setting the stage for greater financial success and fulfillment in life.

Section 4: Insights from experts in psychology, finance, and personal development on the importance of mindset in achieving financial success

Understanding the crucial role of mindset in achieving financial success requires insights from various fields, including psychology, finance, and personal development. In this section, we'll explore perspectives from experts in these domains, shedding light on the significance of mindset in wealth building.

Psychology:
Psychologists have long studied the relationship between mindset and behavior, recognizing the profound impact of thoughts and beliefs on actions and outcomes. According to experts in psychology, individuals with a growth mindset—believing that abilities and intelligence can be developed through dedication and effort—are more likely to persevere in the face of challenges and achieve greater success in various areas of life, including finances.

Dr. Carol Dweck, a renowned psychologist and author of "Mindset: The New Psychology of Success," emphasizes the importance of cultivating a growth mindset for achieving financial success. She argues that those who embrace challenges, persist in the face of setbacks, and see failures as opportunities for growth are better equipped to build wealth and achieve their financial goals.

Finance:
In the realm of finance, experts recognize the interplay

between mindset and financial behavior, highlighting the impact of attitudes and beliefs on financial decision-making and outcomes. According to financial advisors and researchers, individuals with a positive mindset towards money—such as believing in their ability to manage finances effectively, taking calculated risks, and seeking opportunities for growth—are more likely to build wealth and achieve long-term financial stability.

Dr. Daniel Crosby, a psychologist and behavioral finance expert, emphasizes the importance of understanding the psychological biases and emotional factors that influence financial decisions. He argues that by cultivating a mindset of rationality, discipline, and emotional resilience, individuals can navigate the complexities of the financial markets and make sound investment choices that lead to wealth accumulation.

Personal Development:

Personal development experts emphasize the transformative power of mindset in shaping one's life and destiny, including financial success. According to thought leaders in personal development, such as Tony Robbins and Brian Tracy, success is not solely determined by external factors but largely influenced by one's beliefs, attitudes, and habits.

Tony Robbins, a renowned motivational speaker and author, emphasizes the role of mindset in achieving financial abundance. He teaches principles of wealth mastery, including the importance of clarity, focus, and taking massive action towards financial goals. Robbins encourages individuals to cultivate a mindset of abundance, resilience, and resourcefulness to overcome obstacles and create lasting wealth.

In conclusion, insights from experts in psychology, finance, and personal development underscore the critical importance of mindset in achieving financial success. By cultivating a growth mindset, adopting positive attitudes towards money, and mastering the psychological aspects of wealth building, individuals can unlock their full potential and create a life of abundance and prosperity. These insights from experts serve as a guiding light for those seeking to transform their relationship with money and achieve their financial aspirations.

CHAPTER 4: "LEVERAGING OPPORTUNITIES: IDENTIFYING AND CAPITALIZING ON WEALTH-BUILDING VENTURES"

Section 1: In-depth discussion on the different types of wealth-building opportunities

1.1 Entrepreneurship

Entrepreneurship stands as a cornerstone of wealth creation, offering individuals the chance to build businesses from the ground up and capitalize on innovative ideas. It involves taking calculated risks, being resilient in the face of challenges, and leveraging one's skills and resources to create value in the market. Here, we delve into various aspects of entrepreneurship:

1. Startup Ventures: Starting a new business allows individuals to pursue their passions and bring innovative solutions to the market. Whether it's a tech startup disrupting traditional industries or a small local business catering to niche markets, entrepreneurship offers the potential for substantial returns.

2. Scaling Businesses: Scaling a business involves expanding operations to reach a broader audience or enter new markets. This may include opening additional locations, increasing production capacity, or developing new product lines. Scaling allows entrepreneurs to maximize their growth potential and increase profitability over time.

3. Exit Strategies: Successful entrepreneurs often plan exit strategies to realize the value they've created in their businesses. This can involve selling the company to a larger corporation, going public through an initial public offering (IPO), or passing the business down to family members or successors. Careful consideration of exit options is crucial for maximizing returns and ensuring a smooth transition.

1.2 Real Estate Investment

Real estate investment offers a tangible and time-tested avenue for building wealth, with various strategies available to investors. From rental properties to commercial developments, real estate presents opportunities for generating passive income and long-term capital appreciation:

1. Rental Properties: Investing in rental properties involves purchasing residential or commercial real estate and leasing it out to tenants. Rental income provides a steady stream of cash flow, while property appreciation can result in substantial long-term gains. Effective property management and tenant selection are key factors in maximizing returns in this asset class.

2. Fix-and-Flip: Flipping properties involves purchasing distressed or undervalued real estate, renovating or improving it, and selling it for a profit. This strategy requires a keen eye for market trends, understanding of renovation costs, and ability to execute timely renovations to maximize returns.

3. Commercial Real Estate: Investing in commercial properties such as office buildings, retail centers, or industrial warehouses offers opportunities for higher rental yields and potential tax benefits. Commercial leases typically have longer terms and higher rental rates compared to residential properties, making them attractive for investors seeking stable cash flow.

1.3 Stock Market Investing

Investing in the stock market provides individuals with access to a diverse range of publicly traded companies and investment opportunities. While it carries inherent risks, strategic stock market investing can yield significant returns over the long term:

1. Equity Investments: Purchasing shares of publicly traded companies allows investors to participate in the company's growth and profitability. This can be done through individual stock picking or investing in diversified portfolios such as mutual funds or exchange-traded funds (ETFs).

2. Dividend Investing: Dividend investing involves purchasing stocks of companies that regularly distribute dividends to shareholders. These dividends provide a steady stream of passive income, making dividend stocks particularly attractive for income-oriented investors.

3. Index Investing: Index investing entails investing in broad market indices such as the S&P 500 or the Dow Jones Industrial Average. By tracking the performance of the overall market, index investors can benefit from long-term market trends and minimize individual stock risk.

1.4 Alternative Assets

Beyond traditional investment avenues, alternative assets offer unique opportunities for diversification and wealth preservation. These assets often have low correlation with traditional stocks and bonds, providing a hedge against market volatility:

1. Precious Metals: Investing in precious metals such as gold, silver, and platinum offers a safe haven against economic uncertainty and inflation. Precious metals have intrinsic value and are often viewed as a store of wealth during times of market turmoil.

2. Cryptocurrencies: Cryptocurrencies like Bitcoin and Ethereum have emerged as a new asset class with the potential for high returns and significant volatility. While speculative in nature, cryptocurrencies offer diversification benefits and the possibility of substantial gains for investors with a high risk tolerance.

3. Private Equity: Investing in private companies or private equity funds provides access to opportunities not available in public markets. Private equity investments often involve longer holding periods and higher minimum investment requirements but can yield substantial returns through active management and value creation.

By understanding and exploring the various wealth-building opportunities discussed above, individuals can develop a well-rounded investment strategy tailored to their financial goals, risk tolerance, and time horizon. Whether through entrepreneurship, real estate investment, stock market investing, or alternative assets, seizing these opportunities can pave the way toward long-term financial success and wealth accumulation.

Section 2: Examination of the mindset and skills necessary for recognizing and seizing opportunities

2.1 Cultivating Creativity

Creativity is a fundamental trait for recognizing and seizing opportunities. It involves thinking outside the box, generating innovative ideas, and seeing potential where others may not. Cultivating creativity requires:

1. Open-mindedness: Being receptive to new ideas and perspectives allows individuals to explore unconventional solutions and identify unique opportunities.

2. Curiosity: A curious mindset drives exploration and experimentation, leading to breakthroughs and novel approaches to problem-solving.

3. Divergent Thinking: Embracing divergent thinking encourages the generation of multiple solutions to a problem, fostering creativity and innovation.

4. Developing creativity involves engaging in activities such as brainstorming, ideation sessions, and exposure to diverse experiences and viewpoints.

2.2 Fostering Resourcefulness

Resourcefulness is the ability to make the most of available resources and overcome constraints to achieve desired outcomes. It involves:

1. Adaptability: Being adaptable allows individuals to navigate unexpected challenges and pivot when necessary to capitalize on emerging opportunities.

2. Problem-solving Skills: Effective problem-solving skills enable individuals to identify obstacles, devise solutions, and

leverage resources creatively to achieve goals.

3. Resilience: Resilience is crucial for bouncing back from setbacks and maintaining motivation in the face of adversity, essential traits for seizing opportunities amidst uncertainty.

Fostering resourcefulness entails developing a mindset focused on solutions rather than dwelling on limitations, as well as honing skills through practical experience and continuous learning.

2.3 Embracing a Willingness to Learn

A willingness to learn is essential for recognizing and seizing opportunities, as it enables individuals to adapt to evolving circumstances, acquire new knowledge and skills, and remain competitive in dynamic environments. This involves:

1.Continuous Learning: Committing to lifelong learning allows individuals to stay abreast of industry trends, technological advancements, and market developments, providing a competitive edge in identifying and capitalizing on opportunities.

2. Humility: Recognizing one's limitations and being open to feedback and constructive criticism fosters personal growth and development, facilitating the acquisition of new perspectives and insights.

3. Risk-Taking: Embracing calculated risks and stepping outside one's comfort zone is essential for learning and growth, as it exposes individuals to new experiences and opportunities for innovation.

Encouraging a culture of learning within oneself and within organizations promotes adaptability, agility, and a proactive approach to seizing opportunities as they arise.

By fostering creativity, resourcefulness, and a willingness to learn, individuals can cultivate the mindset and skills necessary for recognizing and seizing opportunities effectively. This not only enhances their ability to capitalize on existing opportunities but also enables them to anticipate and create new ones, driving innovation and success in both personal and professional endeavors.

Section 3: Practical guidance on evaluating and prioritizing opportunities

3.1 Assessing Individual Strengths

Before embarking on any opportunity, it's essential to assess individual strengths to determine areas of advantage and potential alignment with opportunities. This involves:

1. Skills Inventory: Conducting a thorough inventory of skills, experiences, and expertise helps individuals identify areas of proficiency and competitive advantage. This could include technical skills, industry knowledge, leadership abilities, and interpersonal skills.

2. Personality Assessment: Understanding one's personality traits, such as introversion/extroversion, risk tolerance, and decision-making style, provides insights into how individuals approach opportunities and make decisions.

3. Passion and Motivation: Assessing personal passions, interests, and values helps individuals align opportunities with their intrinsic motivations, increasing engagement, and commitment to success.

By leveraging individual strengths, individuals can capitalize on opportunities that align with their capabilities and increase the likelihood of achieving success.

3.2 Identifying Interests and Goals

Evaluating personal interests and goals is crucial for selecting opportunities that resonate with individual aspirations and aspirations. This involves:

1. Goal Setting: Establishing clear, measurable goals allows individuals to prioritize opportunities that align with their desired outcomes and long-term objectives. Whether it's financial independence, career advancement, or personal fulfillment, having a clear vision provides a roadmap for decision-making.

2. Passion Alignment: Identifying opportunities that align with personal passions and interests fosters intrinsic motivation and enhances overall satisfaction and fulfillment. Pursuing endeavors that spark enthusiasm increases energy levels, creativity, and resilience in the face of challenges.

3.Lifestyle Considerations: Taking into account lifestyle preferences, such as work-life balance, flexibility, and location independence, helps individuals select opportunities that support their desired lifestyle and overall well-being.

By aligning opportunities with personal interests and goals, individuals can pursue paths that bring fulfillment and satisfaction, enhancing their overall quality of life.

3.3 Evaluating Risk Tolerance

Understanding and assessing risk tolerance is essential for making informed decisions about seizing opportunities. This involves:

1. Risk Assessment: Conducting a thorough evaluation of the potential risks and rewards associated with each opportunity helps individuals assess their risk tolerance and make informed decisions. Factors to consider include financial risk, market volatility, competition, and regulatory considerations.

2. Risk Mitigation Strategies: Developing risk mitigation

strategies, such as diversification, contingency planning, and scenario analysis, helps individuals manage and mitigate potential risks associated with seizing opportunities.

3. Comfort Zone Expansion: Gradually expanding one's comfort zone and taking calculated risks fosters personal growth and resilience, enabling individuals to capitalize on opportunities that may initially seem daunting.

By understanding and evaluating risk tolerance, individuals can make strategic decisions about seizing opportunities that balance potential rewards with acceptable levels of risk.

In conclusion, evaluating and prioritizing opportunities based on individual strengths, interests, and risk tolerance is essential for making informed decisions that align with personal aspirations and objectives. By leveraging strengths, aligning with interests and goals, and assessing risk tolerance, individuals can maximize their chances of success and fulfillment in both personal and professional endeavors.

Section 4: Case studies and interviews with successful entrepreneurs and investors sharing their strategies for identifying and capitalizing on lucrative opportunities

In this section, we delve into real-world examples and insights from accomplished entrepreneurs and investors who have demonstrated exceptional skill in recognizing and seizing lucrative opportunities. Through case studies and interviews, we gain valuable perspectives on their strategies, mindset, and tactics for success.

4.1 Case Study: Entrepreneurial Vision in Action
Case Study: Steve Jobs and Apple Inc.

Steve Jobs, the co-founder of Apple Inc., exemplifies visionary leadership and the ability to identify and capitalize on transformative opportunities. Through his relentless pursuit of innovation and customer-centric approach, Jobs transformed Apple from a niche computer company into one of the world's most valuable and influential technology companies.

Key Strategies and Insights:

1. Customer-Centric Innovation: Jobs emphasized the importance of understanding customer needs and preferences, driving the development of groundbreaking products such as the iPhone, iPad, and iPod.

2. Focus on Design and User Experience: Jobs prioritized elegant design and intuitive user experiences, setting Apple products apart from competitors and fostering brand loyalty.

3. Bold Risk-Taking: Jobs was unafraid to take bold risks and disrupt established industries, such as with the launch of the iPhone, which revolutionized the mobile phone market.

4. Long-Term Vision: Jobs maintained a long-term vision for Apple, continually investing in research and development to anticipate future trends and opportunities.

Through his visionary leadership and innovative spirit, Steve Jobs epitomizes the transformative power of identifying and capitalizing on lucrative opportunities.

4.2 Interview: Investor Insights and Strategies

Interview with Warren Buffett, Chairman and CEO of Berkshire Hathaway

Warren Buffett, renowned investor and philanthropist, shares invaluable insights into his approach to identifying and capitalizing on lucrative investment opportunities.

Key Strategies and Insights:

1. Value Investing: Buffett emphasizes the importance of

value investing, focusing on undervalued companies with strong fundamentals and long-term growth potential.

2. Patience and Discipline: Buffett advocates for patience and discipline in investing, emphasizing the importance of thorough research and avoiding impulsive decisions.

3. Margin of Safety: Buffett seeks investments with a margin of safety, ensuring a sufficient buffer against downside risk and potential losses.

4. Continuous Learning: Buffett emphasizes the importance of continuous learning and intellectual curiosity, staying informed about economic trends, industry dynamics, and company fundamentals.

Through his timeless wisdom and disciplined approach to investing, Warren Buffett provides invaluable lessons on identifying and capitalizing on lucrative opportunities in the financial markets.

By examining case studies and interviews with successful entrepreneurs and investors like Steve Jobs and Warren Buffett, we gain valuable insights into the strategies, mindset, and tactics for recognizing and seizing lucrative opportunities. Their experiences serve as inspiration and guidance for aspiring entrepreneurs and investors seeking to achieve success in their own endeavors.

CHAPTER 5: "THE ART OF WEALTH PRESERVATION: STRATEGIES FOR SUSTAINABLE FINANCIAL SECURITY"

Section 1: Detailed exploration of advanced wealth preservation techniques

Wealth preservation is not merely about accumulating assets; it's also about safeguarding them for current and future generations. In this section, we delve into advanced strategies aimed at protecting your wealth from various risks, optimizing tax efficiency, and ensuring a smooth transition of assets to heirs through succession planning.

1. Asset Protection Strategies:

a. Trust Structures:

Establishing trusts can be a cornerstone of asset protection. Irrevocable trusts, for instance, can shield assets from creditors and legal judgments, as they are no longer considered part of your estate. Moreover, discretionary trusts grant trustees the authority to distribute assets to beneficiaries, providing an additional layer of protection.

b. Limited Liability Entities:

Structuring your assets within limited liability entities such as Limited Liability Companies (LLCs) or Limited Partnerships (LPs) can mitigate personal liability. These entities offer protection by separating business assets from personal assets, shielding the latter in case of business-related liabilities.

c. Domestic and Offshore Asset Protection:

Domestic asset protection trusts (DAPTs) and offshore trusts offer distinct advantages. DAPTs, permitted in select U.S. states, provide statutory protection against creditors. Offshore trusts, on the other hand, offer greater privacy and protection against certain legal claims, albeit subject to international regulations and tax considerations.

2. Tax Planning Strategies:

a. Utilizing Tax-Advantaged Accounts:

Maximizing contributions to tax-advantaged retirement accounts such as 401(k)s, IRAs, or Health Savings Accounts (HSAs) can reduce current taxable income and grow wealth tax-deferred or tax-free, depending on the account type and structure.

b. Capital Gains and Loss Harvesting:

Strategically realizing capital gains and losses can optimize tax liabilities. Timing the sale of assets to offset gains with losses can reduce overall tax obligations, while adhering to tax regulations and considering long-term investment objectives.

c. Estate Tax Mitigation:

For high-net-worth individuals, estate tax planning is crucial.

Techniques such as gifting strategies, establishing trusts, and leveraging life insurance can minimize estate tax burdens, ensuring the preservation of wealth for heirs.

3. Succession Planning Strategies:

a. Comprehensive Estate Planning:

Crafting a comprehensive estate plan involves outlining directives for asset distribution, appointing guardians for dependents, and specifying healthcare and financial powers of attorney. Regular reviews and updates are essential to accommodate changes in personal circumstances or tax laws.

b. Family Limited Partnerships (FLPs) and Family Governance:

FLPs facilitate the transfer of assets to heirs while retaining control within the family. Establishing clear governance structures and communication protocols fosters harmony and continuity across generations, ensuring the sustainability of family wealth.

c. Business Continuity Planning:

For family-owned businesses, succession planning extends beyond asset transfer to ensuring the viability and growth of the enterprise. Implementing strategies such as grooming successors, establishing buy-sell agreements, and securing key person insurance safeguards against disruptions and preserves business value.

In conclusion, advanced wealth preservation encompasses a multifaceted approach integrating asset protection, tax planning, and succession planning strategies. By implementing these techniques in a coordinated manner, individuals can safeguard their wealth, minimize tax liabilities, and facilitate the seamless transfer of assets across generations, thereby ensuring sustainable financial security for themselves and their heirs.

Section 2: Discussion on the role of financial advisors,

estate planners, and other professionals in designing comprehensive wealth preservation strategies

Wealth preservation is a complex endeavor that requires a multidisciplinary approach involving various professionals with specialized expertise. In this section, we explore the pivotal role of financial advisors, estate planners, and other professionals in crafting comprehensive wealth preservation strategies tailored to individual needs and objectives.

1. Financial Advisors:

a. Investment Management:
Financial advisors play a crucial role in managing investment portfolios to achieve long-term growth while mitigating risks. They assess clients' risk tolerance, investment goals, and time horizon to develop personalized investment strategies aligned with wealth preservation objectives.

b. Tax Planning:
Efficient tax planning is integral to wealth preservation. Financial advisors collaborate with tax specialists to optimize tax efficiency by utilizing tax-advantaged accounts, implementing tax-loss harvesting strategies, and structuring investment portfolios in a tax-efficient manner.

c. Risk Management:
Mitigating financial risks is paramount in wealth preservation. Financial advisors conduct comprehensive risk assessments and recommend appropriate insurance products, asset allocation strategies, and risk mitigation techniques to safeguard assets against unforeseen events.

2. Estate Planners:

a. Estate Planning:

Estate planners specialize in creating customized estate plans that facilitate the orderly transfer of assets to heirs while minimizing tax liabilities and avoiding probate. They draft essential estate planning documents such as wills, trusts, and powers of attorney tailored to clients' unique circumstances and preferences.

b. Wealth Transfer Strategies:

Estate planners devise wealth transfer strategies to maximize the value of assets passed on to heirs while minimizing estate and gift taxes. They employ techniques such as lifetime gifting, charitable giving, and generation-skipping trusts to optimize asset distribution and preserve family wealth across generations.

c. Business Succession Planning:

For business owners, estate planners design comprehensive succession plans to ensure the seamless transition of ownership and management to successors. They assess business valuation, draft buy-sell agreements, and implement strategies to minimize tax implications and maintain business continuity.

3. Other Professionals:

a. Legal Advisors:

Legal advisors, including estate planning attorneys and asset protection specialists, provide essential legal guidance in structuring asset protection strategies, drafting legal documents, and navigating complex legal frameworks to safeguard clients' wealth.

b. Accountants:

Accountants play a vital role in tax planning and compliance, providing expert advice on tax optimization strategies, preparing tax returns, and ensuring adherence to regulatory requirements to minimize tax liabilities and preserve wealth.

c. Trust Officers:

Trust officers, employed by financial institutions or trust companies, administer trusts and estate plans, ensuring their proper implementation and compliance with legal and fiduciary standards. They manage trust assets, distribute income to beneficiaries, and facilitate communication among trustees, beneficiaries, and other stakeholders.

In summary, the collaboration of financial advisors, estate planners, and other professionals is indispensable in designing comprehensive wealth preservation strategies. By leveraging their expertise and working collaboratively, individuals can effectively safeguard their assets, optimize tax efficiency, and ensure the seamless transfer of wealth to future generations, thereby achieving sustainable financial security and legacy preservation.

Section 3: Examination of common pitfalls and mistakes to avoid in wealth preservation

Wealth preservation is not just about implementing strategies; it's also about avoiding common pitfalls and mistakes that can erode assets and jeopardize financial security. In this section, we delve into key pitfalls and provide insights on how to mitigate them to ensure effective wealth preservation.

1. Inadequate Insurance Coverage:
a. Underestimating Risks:

One common pitfall is underestimating potential risks and liabilities. Insufficient coverage leaves individuals vulnerable to financial losses resulting from unexpected events such as accidents, illnesses, natural disasters, or legal liabilities.

b. Lack of Diversification:

Relying solely on basic insurance policies may not provide comprehensive protection against all potential risks. It's essential to diversify insurance coverage across different types of policies, including health insurance, life insurance, disability insurance, property and casualty insurance, and liability insurance, to adequately mitigate various risks.

c. Failure to Review and Update Policies:
Insurance needs evolve over time due to changes in personal circumstances, lifestyle, and asset portfolio. Neglecting to periodically review and update insurance policies can lead to gaps in coverage or overpaying for unnecessary coverage, compromising wealth preservation goals.

2. Neglecting Estate Planning:

a. Lack of Documentation:
One of the most critical mistakes is failing to create or update essential estate planning documents such as wills, trusts, and powers of attorney. Without proper documentation, assets may not be distributed according to the individual's wishes, leading to disputes, delays, and potential legal challenges.

b. Inadequate Asset Protection:
Failure to implement asset protection strategies leaves assets vulnerable to creditors, lawsuits, and other legal liabilities. Individuals should work with estate planning professionals to establish trusts, limited liability entities, and other protective measures to safeguard assets against potential risks.

c. Overlooking Tax Planning:
Estate planning should incorporate tax-efficient strategies to minimize estate taxes, gift taxes, and income taxes. Without proper tax planning, a significant portion of the estate may be eroded by unnecessary tax liabilities, diminishing the legacy intended for heirs.

3. Lack of Regular Review and Updates:

a. Failure to Adapt to Changing Circumstances:

Financial and personal circumstances evolve over time, necessitating periodic review and adjustments to wealth preservation strategies. Failing to adapt to changing circumstances may result in outdated strategies that no longer align with current goals and objectives.

b. Ignoring Legislative Changes:

Tax laws, estate planning regulations, and insurance requirements are subject to frequent changes. Individuals must stay informed about legislative developments and consult with professionals to ensure their wealth preservation strategies remain compliant and optimized in light of new regulations.

c. Inadequate Communication:

Effective wealth preservation requires clear communication among family members, advisors, and other stakeholders. Failure to communicate intentions, plans, and expectations may lead to misunderstandings, conflicts, and ultimately, the erosion of family wealth and harmony.

In conclusion, avoiding common pitfalls and mistakes is essential for effective wealth preservation. By proactively addressing risks, updating estate plans, and staying informed about legislative changes, individuals can safeguard their assets, optimize tax efficiency, and ensure the seamless transfer of wealth to future generations, thereby achieving long-term financial security and legacy preservation.

Section 4: Insights from experts in financial planning, law, and wealth management on best practices for ensuring sustainable financial security across generations

In this section, we draw upon the expertise of professionals in financial planning, law, and wealth management to glean insights into best practices for ensuring sustainable financial security across generations. These experts provide valuable perspectives on effective strategies and key considerations for preserving wealth and maintaining financial well-being over the long term.

1. Holistic Financial Planning Approach:

a. Understanding Multigenerational Needs:

Experts emphasize the importance of taking a holistic approach to financial planning that considers the diverse needs and goals of multiple generations within a family. This entails addressing not only immediate financial concerns but also long-term objectives such as retirement planning, education funding, and legacy preservation.

b. Tailoring Strategies to Individual Circumstances:

Financial planning should be personalized to account for unique family dynamics, values, and priorities. By understanding each family member's aspirations, risk tolerance, and life stage, advisors can craft customized strategies that align with their specific needs and objectives.

c. Promoting Financial Literacy and Education:

Empowering family members with financial literacy and education is crucial for long-term financial security. Experts advocate for ongoing dialogue and education about financial concepts, investment principles, and wealth management strategies to foster informed decision-making and responsible stewardship of assets across generations.

2. Comprehensive Estate and Succession Planning:

a. Proactive Wealth Transfer Strategies:

Estate planning professionals stress the importance of proactive wealth transfer strategies to facilitate the orderly transfer of assets to heirs while minimizing tax implications and preserving family wealth. This may involve implementing trusts, gifting strategies, and business succession plans tailored to the family's objectives and circumstances.

b. Establishing Family Governance Structures:

Creating formalized family governance structures can promote transparency, communication, and continuity in wealth management across generations. Experts recommend establishing family councils, constitutions, or advisory boards to facilitate decision-making, resolve conflicts, and preserve family values and legacies.

c. Engaging Professional Advisors:

Collaborating with a team of experienced professionals, including financial advisors, estate planners, tax specialists, and legal advisors, is essential for comprehensive estate and succession planning. By leveraging their collective expertise and guidance, families can navigate complex legal and financial considerations and implement robust wealth preservation strategies.

3. Embracing Philanthropy and Social Responsibility:

a. Incorporating Charitable Giving Strategies:

Integrating philanthropy into wealth management can foster a sense of purpose, unity, and social impact within the family. Experts advocate for incorporating charitable giving strategies, such as donor-advised funds, charitable trusts, or private foundations, to support causes aligned with the family's values and interests while maximizing tax benefits.

b. Instilling Values of Social Responsibility:

Encouraging a culture of social responsibility and ethical stewardship is paramount for ensuring the sustainability of family wealth across generations. By instilling values of integrity, philanthropy, and community engagement, families can nurture a legacy of positive impact and inspire future generations to contribute meaningfully to society.

c. Leveraging Impact Investing Opportunities:

Exploring impact investing opportunities allows families to align their financial goals with their social and environmental values. Experts advocate for integrating environmental, social, and governance (ESG) criteria into investment decisions to generate positive social or environmental outcomes while pursuing financial returns.

In conclusion, insights from experts in financial planning, law, and wealth management underscore the importance of adopting a holistic approach to wealth preservation that encompasses comprehensive financial planning, estate and succession planning, and a commitment to social responsibility. By embracing best practices and engaging professional guidance, families can navigate complex financial challenges, preserve their legacies, and ensure sustainable financial security across generations.

CHAPTER 6: "BUILDING WEALTH WITH PURPOSE: ALIGNING FINANCIAL GOALS WITH PERSONAL VALUES"

Section 1: Deeper Exploration of the Connection Between Wealth and Personal Fulfillment

In this section, we delve into the intricate relationship between wealth and personal fulfillment, exploring how aligning financial goals with personal values can lead to a more meaningful and satisfying life. By examining research on the correlation between money and happiness, we aim to uncover insights that can guide individuals towards a more purpose-driven approach to building wealth.

1.1 Understanding Personal Fulfillment:

Personal fulfillment encompasses a sense of contentment, meaning, and satisfaction derived from one's life experiences, accomplishments, and relationships.

It transcends material wealth and is often deeply intertwined with values, beliefs, and purpose.

1.2 Defining Wealth Beyond Financial Assets:
While financial wealth is a crucial aspect, true wealth encompasses various dimensions such as physical health, mental well-being, relationships, experiences, and contributions to society.

Understanding wealth holistically enables individuals to pursue a balanced and fulfilling life that extends beyond monetary accumulation.

1.3 Research on the Relationship Between Money and Happiness:
Numerous studies have explored the link between money and happiness, offering nuanced insights into how wealth influences subjective well-being.

While income is positively correlated with happiness up to a certain threshold, beyond which the relationship becomes weaker, other factors such as financial security, autonomy, and the ability to meet basic needs play significant roles.

The concept of "hedonic adaptation" suggests that individuals tend to return to a baseline level of happiness despite increases in income, highlighting the transient nature of material possessions in contributing to long-term fulfillment.

Moreover, research indicates that spending money on experiences, meaningful relationships, and altruistic endeavors tends to yield greater happiness compared to materialistic consumption.

1.4 Aligning Financial Goals with Personal Values:
Building wealth with purpose involves aligning financial goals with personal values, aspirations, and priorities.

By reflecting on core values such as integrity, gratitude, compassion, and personal growth, individuals can make intentional decisions about how they earn, save, invest, and spend their money.

Integrating values into financial planning not only fosters a sense of authenticity and fulfillment but also enables individuals to contribute positively to their communities and the world at large.

1.5 Cultivating a Mindful Relationship with Wealth:

Mindfulness practices, such as gratitude journaling, meditation, and conscious spending, can help individuals cultivate a healthier relationship with wealth.

By fostering awareness of their financial habits, values, and motivations, individuals can make more deliberate choices that align with their long-term well-being and aspirations.

1.6 Conclusion:

Recognizing the complex interplay between wealth and personal fulfillment is essential for individuals seeking a more purposeful approach to financial management.

By embracing a holistic definition of wealth, rooted in personal values and well-being, individuals can embark on a journey towards a more fulfilling and meaningful life.

Section 2: Examination of Different Approaches to Defining and Prioritizing Financial Goals

In this section, we explore various methodologies and frameworks for defining and prioritizing financial goals, recognizing that different approaches offer unique insights and benefits to individuals seeking to align their financial objectives with their personal values and aspirations.

2.1 Values-Based Approach to Financial Goal Setting:

The values-based approach to financial goal setting emphasizes the importance of aligning financial objectives with one's core values and beliefs. Rather than focusing solely on monetary outcomes, this approach encourages individuals to reflect on what truly matters to them and to set goals that are in harmony with their deepest aspirations. By identifying and prioritizing values such as family, health, personal growth, community, and environmental stewardship, individuals can craft a financial plan that serves not only their material needs but also their broader vision for a fulfilling and meaningful life. This approach fosters a sense of purpose and authenticity in financial decision-making, empowering individuals to pursue goals that resonate with their innermost desires and priorities.

2.2 SMART Goal Framework:

The SMART goal framework provides a structured approach to setting specific, measurable, achievable, relevant, and time-bound financial objectives. By applying these criteria to their goals, individuals can ensure clarity, focus, and accountability in their pursuit of financial success. Specific goals provide clarity and direction, ensuring that individuals know precisely what they aim to achieve. Measurable goals enable individuals to track their progress and evaluate their success objectively. Achievable goals are realistic and attainable within the given constraints of time, resources, and capabilities. Relevant goals align with one's values, priorities, and long-term aspirations, contributing meaningfully to one's overall well-being and fulfillment. Time-bound goals establish deadlines and milestones, creating a sense of urgency and accountability that propels individuals towards action and achievement. By leveraging the SMART goal framework, individuals can translate their aspirations into concrete plans of action, increasing the likelihood of success and fulfillment in their financial endeavors.

2.3 Integrating Values and SMART Goals:

While the values-based approach and the SMART goal framework offer distinct perspectives on financial goal setting, they are not mutually exclusive. In fact, integrating these approaches can yield synergistic benefits, combining the depth of values-based reflection with the clarity and accountability of SMART goals. By first identifying their core values and aspirations, individuals can then apply the SMART criteria to refine their goals, ensuring that they are specific, measurable, achievable, relevant, and time-bound. This integration enables individuals to pursue financial objectives that are not only aligned with their values but also actionable and attainable in practice. By combining introspection with practical planning, individuals can create a roadmap for financial success that resonates with their deepest desires and aspirations, ultimately leading to a more fulfilling and meaningful life.

2.4 Conclusion:

In conclusion, examining different approaches to defining and prioritizing financial goals provides individuals with valuable tools and perspectives for aligning their financial objectives with their personal values and aspirations. Whether through the values-based approach, the SMART goal framework, or a combination of both, individuals can craft a financial plan that reflects their deepest desires and priorities, leading to greater clarity, fulfillment, and success in their financial journey. By grounding their goals in authenticity, intentionality, and practicality, individuals can embark on a path towards financial well-being and personal fulfillment that honors their unique values and aspirations.

Section 3: Practical exercises and tools for clarifying personal values and aligning financial decisions with long-term aspirations

In this section, we provide individuals with actionable exercises and tools to facilitate the process of clarifying personal values and aligning financial decisions with their long-term aspirations. By engaging in introspective reflection and leveraging practical frameworks, individuals can gain clarity, focus, and confidence in pursuing financial goals that resonate with their deepest values and aspirations.

3.1 Values Clarification Exercises:

Values clarification exercises are powerful tools for individuals to identify and prioritize their core values, which serve as guiding principles in shaping their financial decisions and life choices. Some exercises include:

Values Assessment: Individuals can use self-assessment tools or questionnaires to identify their top values from a predefined list or through open-ended reflection. By examining themes and patterns in their responses, individuals can gain insight into what truly matters to them.

Life Mapping: This exercise involves visually mapping out key life experiences, achievements, and relationships that have shaped one's values and aspirations over time. By reflecting on significant moments and their underlying values, individuals can gain a deeper understanding of what drives them and what they aspire to achieve.

Values Ranking: Individuals can rank their values in order of importance, considering factors such as impact, fulfillment, and alignment with long-term goals. This exercise helps individuals prioritize their values and make decisions that are consistent with their highest priorities.

3.2 Financial Goal Setting Tools:

Once individuals have clarified their values, they can leverage various tools and frameworks to translate their aspirations into actionable financial goals. Some practical tools include:

Goal Setting Worksheets: These worksheets provide a structured framework for individuals to define their financial goals in specific, measurable, achievable, relevant, and time-bound terms (SMART criteria). By breaking down goals into actionable steps and setting deadlines, individuals can create a roadmap for success.

Budgeting and Financial Planning Apps: Budgeting apps and financial planning software offer features such as expense tracking, goal setting, and financial projections. By inputting their financial goals and tracking their progress over time, individuals can stay accountable and make informed decisions aligned with their values.

Vision Boards and Visualization Exercises: Visual tools such as vision boards or visualization exercises allow individuals to create a tangible representation of their financial goals and aspirations. By visualizing their desired outcomes and experiences, individuals can strengthen their motivation and focus on achieving their goals.

3.3 Integration of Values and Goals:
Integrating personal values into financial goal setting involves aligning each goal with the values that matter most to the individual. This process may include:

Values-Based Goal Evaluation: Before finalizing financial goals, individuals can assess each goal against their core values to ensure alignment and relevance. Goals that resonate with one's values are more likely to inspire motivation and commitment.

Values-Centered Decision Making: In making financial decisions, individuals can consider how each option aligns with their values and contributes to their long-term well-being and fulfillment. By prioritizing values over short-term gratification, individuals can make choices that are consistent with their authentic selves.

Regular Reflection and Adjustment: Financial goals and values may evolve over time, necessitating regular reflection and adjustment. By revisiting their values and goals periodically, individuals can ensure that their financial plan remains aligned with their evolving aspirations and priorities.

3.4 Conclusion:

In conclusion, practical exercises and tools for clarifying personal values and aligning financial decisions with long-term aspirations empower individuals to live authentically and pursue financial goals that resonate with their deepest desires. By engaging in values clarification exercises, leveraging financial goal setting tools, and integrating values into decision making, individuals can create a roadmap for financial success that reflects their unique values, aspirations, and priorities. Through intentional reflection and action, individuals can cultivate a sense of purpose, fulfillment, and abundance in their financial journey.

Section 4: Case Studies and Testimonials Demonstrating the Transformative Power of Aligning Financial Goals with Personal Values

In this section, we present case studies and testimonials from individuals who have embarked on a journey of aligning their financial goals with their personal values. These stories illustrate the profound impact that intentional, values-driven wealth-building can have on individuals' lives, showcasing the transformative power of living authentically and pursuing financial goals that are aligned with one's deepest aspirations.

4.1 Case Study: Sarah's Journey to Financial Freedom and Philanthropy

Sarah, a successful business executive, found herself feeling unfulfilled despite her material success. After a period of introspection, she realized that her pursuit of wealth had been driven primarily by external expectations rather than her own values. Inspired to make a change, Sarah reevaluated her financial goals and identified her passion for philanthropy as a core value. With a renewed sense of purpose, she shifted her focus towards building wealth with the intention of making a positive impact on causes she cared about deeply.

Over time, Sarah implemented a values-based financial plan

hat prioritized charitable giving, sustainable investing, and conscious spending. She established a donor-advised fund to support organizations aligned with her values, volunteered her time to causes she was passionate about, and sought out investment opportunities that aligned with her environmental and social values. As Sarah's wealth grew, so did her sense of fulfillment and purpose. She found joy in using her resources to make a meaningful difference in the world, ultimately realizing that true wealth lies not in accumulation but in contribution.

4.2 Testimonial: John's Journey to Financial Independence and Family Well-Being

John, a devoted husband and father, had always dreamed of providing financial security and stability for his family. However, his demanding career left him feeling disconnected from his loved ones and overwhelmed by financial pressures. Determined to prioritize his family's well-being and quality of life, John embarked on a journey of aligning his financial goals with his personal values.

Through intentional goal setting and financial planning, John gradually transitioned to a more flexible work arrangement that allowed him to spend more time with his family. He prioritized experiences over material possessions, investing in family vacations, educational opportunities for his children, and meaningful time spent together. By aligning his financial decisions with his values of family, balance, and well-being, John found a renewed sense of joy and fulfillment in his relationships and his life overall.

4.3 Case Study: Maria's Journey to Financial Empowerment and Community Impact

Maria, a social worker passionate about empowering marginalized communities, faced financial challenges as she struggled to make ends meet on a modest income. Despite limited resources, Maria remained committed to her values of social justice and community empowerment. Determined to create positive change, Maria sought out opportunities to leverage her skills and resources to make a difference.

Through networking and community partnerships, Maria discovered creative ways to maximize her impact without relying solely on financial resources. She volunteered her time to mentor youth, advocate for policy change, and organize grassroots initiatives. By harnessing her passion and expertise, Maria inspired others to join her cause and effect meaningful change in her community. While her financial situation remained modest, Maria found fulfillment and purpose in her ability to make a tangible difference in the lives of others, proving that wealth is not measured solely in dollars but in the positive impact we have on the world around us.

4.4 Testimonial: David's Journey to Financial Wellness and Personal Growth

David, a young professional, found himself overwhelmed by debt and financial uncertainty as he navigated the challenges of early adulthood. Determined to take control of his financial future and live a life aligned with his values, David embarked on a journey of financial wellness and personal growth.

Through education, discipline, and perseverance, David developed a budgeting and debt repayment plan that allowed him to regain control of his finances and build a foundation for long-term success. He prioritized his mental and physical health, investing in self-care practices and personal development activities that nurtured his well-being and resilience. As David's financial situation stabilized and his confidence grew, he began to explore new opportunities for career advancement and personal fulfillment, ultimately realizing that true wealth encompasses not only financial security but also personal growth, fulfillment, and well-being.

4.5 Conclusion:

These case studies and testimonials offer compelling examples of the transformative power of aligning financial goals with personal values. Through intentional reflection, goal setting, and action, individuals can create a life of purpose, meaning, and fulfillment, where wealth is measured not only in monetary terms but also in the positive impact we have on ourselves, our loved ones, and the world around us. By prioritizing values over materialism and living authentically, individuals can unlock the true potential of their wealth-building journey and create a legacy that extends far beyond financial success.

CHAPTER 7: "THE ROLE OF RELATIONSHIPS: LEVERAGING NETWORKS FOR WEALTH CREATION"

Section 1: Exploration of the importance of relationships and networking in building wealth and opportunities

In the dynamic landscape of wealth creation, the significance of relationships and networking cannot be overstated. This section delves into the pivotal role that relationships play in the journey towards building wealth and seizing opportunities.

1. Foundational Pillars of Success:

Relationships form the cornerstone of success in various spheres of life, including business, entrepreneurship, and career advancement. By fostering meaningful connections with individuals across diverse backgrounds, industries, and expertise areas, individuals can tap into a wealth of knowledge, resources, and opportunities.

2. Access to Opportunities:

Networking opens doors to a plethora of opportunities that may otherwise remain inaccessible. Whether it's discovering potential investment ventures, accessing new markets, or forging strategic partnerships, well-nurtured relationships serve as conduits for unlocking avenues for growth and wealth accumulation.

3. Information and Insights:

Within professional networks, individuals gain access to valuable information and insights that are instrumental in making informed decisions. Whether it's staying abreast of industry trends, market developments, or emerging technologies, the exchange of information within networks empowers individuals to anticipate changes and adapt their strategies accordingly.

4. Mentorship and Guidance:

Relationships often provide a platform for mentorship and guidance, where seasoned professionals impart wisdom, share experiences, and offer advice to those navigating their journey towards wealth creation. Through mentorship, individuals can avoid pitfalls, capitalize on opportunities, and accelerate their progress towards achieving their financial goals.

5. Collaboration and Synergy:

Collaborative endeavors thrive within well-connected networks, where individuals pool their resources, skills, and expertise to achieve common objectives. By fostering a spirit of collaboration, networks facilitate the creation of synergies that drive innovation, productivity, and value creation, ultimately contributing to wealth accumulation for all involved parties.

6. Personal and Professional Growth:

Beyond tangible benefits, relationships foster personal and professional growth by exposing individuals to diverse perspectives, challenging their assumptions, and expanding their horizons. Through meaningful interactions with peers, mentors, and industry leaders, individuals cultivate essential skills such as communication, negotiation, and leadership, which are indispensable assets in the pursuit of wealth creation.

7. Building Trust and Credibility:

Trust is the bedrock upon which successful relationships are built. By consistently demonstrating integrity, reliability, and authenticity in their interactions, individuals cultivate trust and credibility within their networks. These qualities not only enhance their reputation but also serve as catalysts for fostering enduring partnerships and unlocking new opportunities for wealth creation.

In essence, relationships and networking serve as catalysts for wealth creation by providing access to opportunities, information, mentorship, collaboration, personal growth, and trust-building. As individuals navigate the intricate landscape of wealth accumulation, investing in nurturing and expanding their networks emerges as a strategic imperative for unlocking the full spectrum of possibilities and realizing their financial aspirations.

Section 2: Discussion on building and maintaining professional and personal networks

Building and maintaining networks, whether professional or personal, requires deliberate effort, strategic communication, and genuine relationship-building. This section explores various strategies for effectively cultivating and sustaining meaningful connections.

1.Identifying Common Ground:

Effective networking begins with identifying common ground and shared interests. Whether it's attending industry events, joining professional associations, or participating in online forums, individuals should seek out opportunities to connect with like-minded individuals who share their passions, goals, or areas of expertise.

2. Authenticity and Genuine Interest:
Authenticity forms the bedrock of meaningful relationships. Individuals should approach networking with a genuine interest in getting to know others, listening attentively to their perspectives, and offering support or assistance whenever possible. Authentic connections are built on sincerity, trust, and mutual respect, laying the foundation for long-lasting partnerships.

3. Effective Communication Skills:
Effective communication lies at the heart of successful networking. Individuals should hone their communication skills, including active listening, concise articulation of ideas, and the ability to convey empathy and understanding. By fostering clear and meaningful dialogues, individuals can forge deeper connections and leave a lasting impression on their peers.

4. Value Exchange and Reciprocity:
Networking is a two-way street, grounded in the principle of value exchange and reciprocity. Individuals should strive to add value to their connections by offering insights, resources, or assistance that address their needs or challenges. By nurturing a culture of reciprocity within their networks, individuals foster goodwill and cultivate mutually beneficial relationships.

5. Consistency and Follow-Up:
Building and maintaining networks require consistent effort and follow-up. Individuals should proactively nurture their connections by staying in touch, expressing appreciation, and following up on previous interactions. Whether it's sending a personalized email, scheduling a follow-up meeting, or connecting on social media platforms, consistent engagement reinforces the strength of relationships over time.

6. Diversifying Networks:

To maximize the breadth and depth of their networks, individuals should actively seek out diverse perspectives and experiences. Building relationships with individuals from different industries, cultural backgrounds, and demographic groups not only expands one's worldview but also unlocks new opportunities for collaboration, innovation, and growth.

7. Seeking Mentorship and Guidance:

Mentorship plays a pivotal role in personal and professional development. Individuals should seek out mentors within their networks who can offer guidance, wisdom, and support based on their own experiences. By cultivating mentor-mentee relationships, individuals gain invaluable insights, navigate challenges more effectively, and accelerate their journey towards achieving their goals.

8. Adapting to Virtual Networking:

In an increasingly digital world, virtual networking has become a prevalent mode of connecting with others. Individuals should leverage online platforms, social media networks, and virtual events to expand their reach, engage with diverse audiences, and forge meaningful connections across geographical boundaries. Adapting to the nuances of virtual networking allows individuals to stay connected and leverage opportunities in an ever-evolving landscape.

By adopting these strategies for effective communication and relationship building, individuals can build and maintain robust professional and personal networks that serve as catalysts for wealth creation, personal growth, and fulfillment. Through consistent effort, genuine engagement, and a commitment to adding value, individuals can unlock the full potential of their networks and harness the collective power of collaboration and connection.

Section 3: Examination of how mentorship, partnerships, and collaborations can accelerate wealth creation

Mentorship, partnerships, and collaborations are potent vehicles for accelerating wealth creation by leveraging the collective knowledge, resources, and networks of multiple stakeholders. This section delves into the transformative impact of mentorship, strategic partnerships, and collaborative endeavors on the journey towards financial prosperity.

Mentorship as a Catalyst for Growth:

Mentorship plays a pivotal role in guiding individuals along their path to wealth creation. Experienced mentors offer invaluable insights, advice, and support based on their own successes and failures, helping mentees navigate challenges, identify opportunities, and make informed decisions. By tapping into the wisdom and expertise of mentors, individuals can expedite their learning curve, avoid costly mistakes, and fast-track their progress towards achieving their financial goals.

Strategic Partnerships for Synergy and Scale:

Strategic partnerships enable individuals to pool their resources, expertise, and networks to achieve shared objectives and unlock new opportunities for growth. Whether it's forming alliances with complementary businesses, collaborating with industry leaders, or forging strategic alliances with key stakeholders, partnerships facilitate synergistic relationships that drive innovation, expand market reach, and enhance competitive advantage. By harnessing the collective strengths of partners, individuals can accelerate their pace of wealth creation and achieve sustainable success in a rapidly evolving landscape.

Collaborative Endeavors Driving Innovation:

Collaborations foster a culture of innovation by bringing together diverse perspectives, skill sets, and resources to tackle complex challenges and capitalize on emerging opportunities.

Whether it's cross-disciplinary collaborations, joint ventures, or innovation ecosystems, collaborative endeavors spark creativity, fuel ideation, and catalyze the development of disruptive solutions that have the potential to revolutionize industries and create new avenues for wealth creation. By fostering a spirit of collaboration, individuals can tap into the collective intelligence of their networks and drive transformative change that generates significant value and competitive advantage.

Access to New Markets and Opportunities:

Mentorship, partnerships, and collaborations provide individuals with access to new markets, customer segments, and distribution channels that may have been previously out of reach. By leveraging the networks and resources of their mentors, partners, and collaborators, individuals can expand their market footprint, penetrate untapped demographics, and capitalize on emerging trends and consumer preferences. Access to new markets and opportunities amplifies revenue streams, diversifies income sources, and accelerates wealth creation by unlocking previously inaccessible growth avenues.

Risk Mitigation and Resilience:

Mentorship, partnerships, and collaborations serve as a form of risk mitigation by spreading risks across multiple stakeholders and diversifying exposure to potential pitfalls. Through the collective expertise, resources, and support of mentors, partners, and collaborators, individuals can navigate uncertainties, withstand market fluctuations, and adapt to changing conditions with greater resilience and agility. By sharing both the risks and rewards of collaborative endeavors, individuals can safeguard their investments, preserve wealth, and position themselves for long-term success in an increasingly volatile and uncertain environment.

In summary, mentorship, partnerships, and collaborations are indispensable drivers of wealth creation, offering individuals access to mentorship, strategic alliances, collaborative opportunities, market expansion, risk mitigation, and resilience. By harnessing the power of collective intelligence, expertise, and networks, individuals can accelerate their journey towards financial prosperity, capitalize on emerging opportunities, and create lasting value that transcends individual achievements.

Section 4: Case studies and anecdotes highlighting the role of relationships in the success stories of entrepreneurs and investors.

In this section, we'll delve into illuminating case studies and anecdotes that underscore the pivotal role of relationships in the journeys of entrepreneurs and investors. These real-life examples vividly demonstrate how strategic networking, mentorship, and collaborative partnerships have propelled individuals towards extraordinary success and accelerated wealth creation.

Case Study 1: Leveraging Mentorship for Innovation and Growth

*Jake, a budding entrepreneur in the tech industry, had a bold vision to revolutionize the way people interacted with fitness and health data. However, navigating the complexities of startup growth proved daunting. Through a serendipitous encounter at a networking event, Jake connected with a seasoned entrepreneur, Emma, who had successfully scaled multiple tech startups. Recognizing Jake's passion and potential, Emma took him under her wing, offering invaluable mentorship, strategic guidance, and access to her extensive network of investors and industry influencers. With Emma's mentorship, Jake honed his business strategy, refined his product offerings, and secured significant funding from venture capitalists impressed by Emma's endorsement. Today, Jake's startup stands as a market leader in fitness technology, thanks in large part to the transformative power of mentorship and relationship-building.

Case Study 2: The Impact of Strategic Partnerships on Market Expansion

*Samantha, an ambitious entrepreneur in the food and beverage industry, dreamed of introducing her artisanal gourmet products to international markets. Recognizing the challenges of global expansion, Samantha sought out strategic partnerships with established distributors and retailers in key target regions. Through diligent networking and relationship-building efforts, Samantha secured partnerships with leading distributors in Europe and Asia, gaining access to an extensive network of retailers and consumers. These strategic alliances not only facilitated market entry but also provided invaluable insights into local preferences, regulatory requirements, and distribution channels. Leveraging her partnerships, Samantha successfully launched her products in multiple countries, achieving rapid sales growth and establishing a global brand presence. The power of strategic partnerships propelled Samantha's business to new heights, enabling her to realize her vision of international expansion.

Case Study 3: Collaborative Ventures Driving Innovation and Impact

*Tom and Lisa, two entrepreneurs with a shared passion for environmental sustainability, joined forces to tackle the pressing issue of plastic waste pollution. Leveraging their respective expertise in product design and waste management, Tom and Lisa co-founded a startup focused on developing biodegradable alternatives to single-use plastics. Recognizing the importance of collaboration, they forged partnerships with research institutions, environmental organizations, and government agencies. Through collaborative research efforts and knowledge-sharing initiatives, Tom and Lisa's startup developed groundbreaking biopolymer technology that offered a sustainable solution to plastic waste. Their collaborative venture garnered widespread attention and support, attracting investment from impact-focused funds and corporate partners committed to sustainability. Together, Tom and Lisa's startup achieved significant milestones in reducing plastic pollution

and promoting environmental stewardship, demonstrating the transformative potential of collaborative ventures driven by shared values and relationships.

These case studies and anecdotes vividly illustrate the profound impact of relationships on the success stories of entrepreneurs and investors. Whether through mentorship, strategic partnerships, or collaborative ventures, individuals can harness the power of their networks to overcome challenges, seize opportunities, and achieve remarkable feats of innovation, growth, and impact. In a rapidly evolving business landscape, cultivating meaningful relationships isn't just a strategy—it's a catalyst for transformative change and enduring success.

CHAPTER 8: "EMBRACING FAILURE: LESSONS FROM SETBACKS ON THE PATH TO SUCCESS"

Section 1: Examination of the Role of Failure and Adversity in the Journey to Financial Success

In this section, we delve into the intricate relationship between failure, adversity, and financial success. Drawing upon psychological research and real-world examples, we uncover the nuanced dynamics that underlie these seemingly contradictory elements on the path to achievement.

1.1 The Psychology of Failure:

Failure, often perceived as a setback or defeat, holds significant psychological implications for individuals. Psychologists have long studied the effects of failure on human behavior and cognition. Contrary to popular belief, failure is not solely a negative experience; rather, it serves as a crucial catalyst for growth and development.

Research in cognitive psychology suggests that individuals who view failure as a learning opportunity exhibit greater resilience and adaptability in the face of challenges. This growth mindset, as coined by psychologist Carol Dweck, emphasizes the belief that abilities can be developed through dedication and hard work, rather than being fixed traits. Embracing failure within this framework fosters a mindset conducive to innovation and progress.

Furthermore, failure activates regions of the brain associated with motivation and learning. Neuroscientific studies have shown that setbacks trigger the release of dopamine, a neurotransmitter linked to reward and reinforcement. Consequently, individuals may experience a surge in motivation following failure, propelling them towards greater determination and perseverance.

1.2 Real-World Examples:

Numerous real-world examples illustrate the transformative power of failure on the journey to financial success. Silicon Valley, renowned for its entrepreneurial spirit, abounds with stories of startups that emerged stronger from initial failures.

Take, for instance, the case of Steve Jobs, co-founder of Apple Inc. Following his ousting from the company he helped create, Jobs experienced a profound setback in his career. However, rather than succumbing to defeat, he leveraged this failure as an opportunity for introspection and growth. Subsequently, Jobs returned to Apple with renewed vigor, spearheading the development of revolutionary products such as the iPod, iPhone, and iPad, ultimately reshaping the landscape of technology and amassing immense wealth in the process.

Similarly, the journey of J.K. Rowling, author of the Harry Potter series, exemplifies the resilience forged in the crucible of failure. Prior to achieving literary stardom, Rowling faced a litany of rejections from publishers and endured periods of financial hardship. Yet, undeterred by setbacks, she persisted in her pursuit of creative expression. Today, Rowling stands as one of the wealthiest authors in the world, her tales of wizardry captivating millions of readers worldwide.

These examples underscore the pivotal role of failure in the trajectory of financial success. By embracing setbacks as stepping stones rather than stumbling blocks, individuals can harness the transformative potential of adversity to propel themselves towards greater heights of achievement.

In conclusion, the examination of failure and adversity unveils a paradoxical truth: within the crucible of setbacks lies the seeds of success. By cultivating a growth mindset and drawing inspiration from real-world exemplars, individuals can navigate the turbulent waters of failure with resilience and determination, ultimately forging a path towards financial prosperity.

Section 2: Discussion on Reframing Failure as a Learning Opportunity and Catalyst for Growth

In this section, we delve deeper into the transformative potential of failure when reframed as a catalyst for growth and a valuable learning opportunity. Through examining various perspectives from psychology, education, and personal development, we explore strategies for embracing failure as a stepping stone towards success.

2.1 Shifting Perspectives:

The first step in leveraging failure for growth is to shift one's perspective from viewing it as a defeat to seeing it as a valuable learning experience. This reframing process involves challenging the negative connotations associated with failure and reconizing it as an essential part of the journey towards mastery and achievement.

Psychological research suggests that individuals who adopt a growth mindset are more resilient in the face of failure. By believing that abilities can be developed through effort and perseverance, individuals are better equipped to navigate setbacks and setbacks with resilience and determination.

Educational theories such as constructivism emphasize the importance of experiential learning and reflection in the acquisition of knowledge and skills. From this perspective, failure serves as a natural part of the learning process, providing valuable feedback that informs future actions and decision-making.

2.2 Cultivating Resilience:

Central to reframing failure as a learning opportunity is the cultivation of resilience – the ability to bounce back from adversity stronger than before. Resilience encompasses a combination of psychological factors, including optimism, self-efficacy, and adaptive coping strategies.

One effective strategy for building resilience is cognitive reappraisal, whereby individuals reinterpret setbacks in a more positive light. Instead of dwelling on perceived failures, they focus on the lessons learned and the opportunities for growth that emerge from adversity.

Furthermore, fostering a supportive environment characterized by trust, empathy, and encouragement can bolster resilience in the face of failure. Whether in educational settings, workplaces, or personal relationships, a culture that celebrates effort and perseverance fosters a sense of belonging and empowerment, enabling individuals to weather the storms of failure with resilience and grace.

2.3 Embracing the Growth Mindset:

At the heart of reframing failure as a catalyst for growth lies the concept of the growth mindset, as pioneered by psychologist Carol Dweck. According to Dweck, individuals with a growth mindset believe that intelligence and abilities are not fixed traits but can be developed through dedication and hard work.

By embracing the growth mindset, individuals view failure not as evidence of their limitations but as an opportunity to stretch beyond their comfort zones and expand their potential. This mindset shift fosters a sense of empowerment and agency, empowering individuals to persevere in the face of adversity and pursue their goals with passion and determination.

In conclusion, reframing failure as a learning opportunity and catalyst for growth requires a fundamental shift in perspective and mindset. By embracing failure as an integral part of the journey towards success, individuals can cultivate resilience, adaptability, and perseverance, ultimately unlocking their full potential and achieving their dreams.

Section 3: Strategies for Resilience and Bouncing Back from Setbacks

In this section, we explore practical strategies for building resilience and bouncing back from setbacks. Drawing upon insights from psychology, personal development, and leadership, we highlight the importance of self-reflection, adaptability, and perseverance in navigating the challenges of failure.

3.1 Self-Reflection:

Self-reflection plays a pivotal role in the process of bouncing back from setbacks. It involves taking a step back to examine one's thoughts, emotions, and behaviors in response to failure, with the aim of gaining insights and learning from the experience.

One effective strategy for self-reflection is journaling. By writing down their thoughts and feelings, individuals can gain clarity and perspective on the situation, identify patterns of thinking or behavior that may be hindering their progress, and formulate constructive strategies for moving forward.

Additionally, seeking feedback from trusted mentors, peers, or coaches can provide valuable perspectives and insights that may not be apparent to the individual alone. By soliciting diverse viewpoints and engaging in open dialogue, individuals can broaden their understanding of the situation and uncover new possibilities for growth and development.

Furthermore, practicing mindfulness and self-compassion can help individuals cultivate a non-judgmental awareness of their experiences and emotions, enabling them to navigate setbacks with greater resilience and self-acceptance.

3.2 Adaptability:

Adaptability is another essential quality for bouncing back from setbacks. In today's rapidly changing world, the ability to pivot and adjust course in response to unforeseen challenges is crucial for success.

One strategy for fostering adaptability is to adopt a flexible mindset. Rather than rigidly adhering to preconceived plans or expectations, individuals can embrace uncertainty and change as opportunities for innovation and growth. This may involve reassessing goals, revising strategies, or exploring alternative pathways to success.

Moreover, cultivating a diverse skill set and a willingness to learn new things can enhance adaptability in the face of adversity. By continuously seeking out opportunities for personal and professional development, individuals can position themselves to thrive in dynamic and unpredictable environments.

3.3 Perseverance:

Perseverance, or the steadfast pursuit of goals in the face of obstacles, is a key determinant of success in overcoming setbacks. It involves maintaining a resilient attitude and staying committed to one's aspirations, even in the face of adversity.

One strategy for fostering perseverance is to cultivate a sense of purpose and intrinsic motivation. By aligning their goals with their values and passions, individuals can tap into a deep reservoir of inner drive and determination that sustains them through difficult times.

Additionally, breaking goals down into manageable tasks and milestones can make them feel more attainable and less daunting. By focusing on small, incremental progress, individuals can maintain momentum and stay motivated, even in the face of setbacks or challenges.

Furthermore, building a strong support network of friends, family, mentors, and colleagues can provide invaluable encouragement and accountability during times of adversity. By surrounding themselves with positive influences and seeking support when needed, individuals can draw strength from their connections and persevere in the pursuit of their dreams.

In conclusion, resilience is a skill that can be cultivated through self-reflection, adaptability, and perseverance. By adopting these strategies and embracing failure as an opportunity for growth, individuals can bounce back from setbacks stronger and more resilient than before, ultimately achieving their goals and realizing their full potential.

Section 4: Inspirational Stories of Individuals Who Turned Failure into Success

In this section, we delve into the inspiring journeys of individuals who transformed failure into triumph, emerging stronger and more resilient from adversity. These stories serve as powerful reminders of the transformative potential inherent in setbacks, illustrating how resilience, perseverance, and a growth mindset can pave the way for success.

4.1 The Story of Oprah Winfrey:

Oprah Winfrey, one of the most influential media moguls of our time, faced numerous setbacks and challenges on her path to success. Born into poverty and raised in a tumultuous environment, Oprah endured childhood trauma and adversity, including sexual abuse and family instability.

Despite these early hardships, Oprah refused to be defined by her circumstances. Drawing upon her innate resilience and determination, she pursued a career in media, eventually landing a role as a news anchor and talk show host. However, her initial foray into television was met with failure, as her show was canceled due to low ratings.

Undeterred, Oprah persevered and launched "The Oprah Winfrey Show," which quickly became a cultural phenomenon, propelling her to unprecedented levels of success and influence. Through her platform, Oprah has empowered millions of viewers worldwide with her message of hope, inspiration, and personal growth.

Oprah's story exemplifies the transformative power of resilience and perseverance in the face of adversity. By refusing to be defined by her past or limited by her circumstances, she turned her setbacks into stepping stones, ultimately achieving unparalleled success and impact.

4.2 The Journey of Walt Disney:

Walt Disney, the visionary behind the iconic Disney empire, experienced his fair share of failures and setbacks on the road to success. Early in his career, Disney faced bankruptcy and the loss of his first animation studio, Laugh-O-Gram Films, due to financial difficulties.

Rather than succumbing to defeat, Disney saw these setbacks as opportunities for growth and innovation. Armed with a relentless drive and a steadfast belief in his creative vision, he persevered, founding the Disney Brothers Studio and introducing groundbreaking innovations in animation, including synchronized sound and Technicolor.

Despite facing numerous obstacles and setbacks, Disney's unwavering determination and creative genius propelled him to unprecedented success, revolutionizing the entertainment industry and leaving behind a timeless legacy that continues to inspire generations.

Disney's story serves as a testament to the power of resilience, creativity, and perseverance in the face of adversity. By embracing failure as a natural part of the creative process and refusing to give up on his dreams, Disney transformed his setbacks into opportunities for greatness, ultimately leaving an indelible mark on the world.

4.3 The Triumph of J.K. Rowling:

J.K. Rowling, the beloved author of the Harry Potter series, experienced her fair share of rejection and setbacks before achieving literary stardom. Struggling as a single mother living on welfare, Rowling faced countless rejections from publishers who doubted the commercial viability of her manuscripts.

Despite these initial setbacks, Rowling refused to abandon her dreams of becoming a published author. Drawing upon her love of storytelling and her unwavering belief in the transformative power of imagination, she continued to persevere, pouring her heart and soul into her writing.

Finally, after years of rejection and adversity, Rowling's perseverance paid off when Bloomsbury Publishing agreed to publish her debut novel, "Harry Potter and the Philosopher's Stone." The rest, as they say, is history, as the Harry Potter series went on to become a global phenomenon, captivating millions of readers and inspiring a generation of fans.

Rowling's story is a powerful reminder of the resilience and determination required to turn failure into success. By refusing to be deterred by rejection or discouraged by setbacks, Rowling embraced her failures as opportunities for growth and self-discovery, ultimately realizing her dreams and leaving behind a literary legacy that will endure for generations to come.

In conclusion, the inspirational stories of individuals like Oprah Winfrey, Walt Disney, and J.K. Rowling serve as powerful reminders of the transformative potential inherent in setbacks. Through resilience, perseverance, and a growth mindset, these individuals turned failure into success, emerging stronger and more resilient from adversity. Their stories inspire us to embrace failure as a natural part of the journey towards success, recognizing that it is not the end of the road but merely a detour on the path to greatness.

CHAPTER 9: "ETHICAL WEALTH: NAVIGATING MORALITY AND MONEY"

Section 1: Exploration of the Intersection between Ethics, Morality, and Wealth Creation

In the modern world, the intersection between ethics, morality, and wealth creation has become increasingly complex and consequential. This section delves into the intricate dynamics that govern this intersection, highlighting the ethical implications of various financial decisions and practices.

Understanding Ethics and Morality:

Before delving into the ethical dimensions of wealth creation, it's crucial to define the terms "ethics" and "morality." Ethics refers to the set of principles or values that govern an individual's behavior or the conduct of a group. Morality, on the other hand, pertains to the distinction between right and wrong conduct and the principles that guide human behavior in making those distinctions. While ethics often refers to a broader societal or professional context, morality tends to be more personal and subjective.

Wealth Creation and Ethical Dilemmas:

The pursuit of wealth inevitably raises ethical dilemmas, as individuals and organizations navigate decisions that impact not only their financial prosperity but also the well-being of others and the environment. For instance, considerations such as labor practices, environmental sustainability, and social responsibility often come into conflict with profit motives.

Labor Practices:

One of the most significant ethical considerations in wealth creation is the treatment of labor. This encompasses issues such as fair wages, working conditions, and labor rights. Companies may face dilemmas regarding outsourcing to regions with lower labor standards or exploiting workers to maximize profits. Ethical wealth creation necessitates a commitment to fair labor practices, ensuring that workers are treated with dignity and respect.

Environmental Sustainability:

The environmental impact of wealth creation is another critical ethical concern. Industries such as manufacturing, energy production, and agriculture often contribute to pollution, deforestation, and climate change. Ethical wealth creation involves adopting sustainable practices that minimize environmental harm, investing in renewable energy, and mitigating carbon emissions.

Social Responsibility:

Beyond economic considerations, ethical wealth creation entails a commitment to social responsibility. This includes giving back to communities, supporting charitable causes, and addressing social inequalities. Companies are increasingly expected to prioritize social impact alongside financial profitability, recognizing their role as stakeholders in society.

Financial Decision-Making:

At an individual level, financial decision-making also raises ethical questions. Choices regarding investments, consumption patterns, and philanthropy reflect personal values and moral principles. For instance, investing in companies with unethical business practices may yield financial returns but could contribute to social harm. Ethical investors prioritize environmental, social, and governance (ESG) factors, aligning their investments with their values.

Navigating Ethical Dilemmas:

In navigating the intersection between ethics, morality, and wealth creation, individuals and organizations must grapple with complex dilemmas and trade-offs. Balancing financial objectives with ethical considerations requires careful deliberation and a commitment to principles of integrity and social responsibility. Engaging in transparent dialogue, seeking diverse perspectives, and adhering to ethical frameworks can help guide decision-making in morally ambiguous situations.

Conclusion:

The exploration of ethics, morality, and wealth creation underscores the interconnectedness of economic prosperity, social responsibility, and ethical conduct. By recognizing the ethical implications of financial decisions and practices, individuals and organizations can strive towards a more equitable and sustainable approach to wealth creation, fostering positive outcomes for both stakeholders and society at large.

Section 2: Discussion on the importance of integrity, transparency, and social responsibility in wealth accumulation

Integrity, transparency, and social responsibility are foundational principles that play a crucial role in the process of wealth accumulation. In this section, we delve into the significance of these values and their impact on individuals, organizations, and society as a whole.

1. Integrity in Wealth Accumulation:

Integrity forms the bedrock of ethical behavior in wealth accumulation. It entails honesty, sincerity, and adherence to moral principles, even in the face of temptations or pressures to compromise. Individuals and organizations with integrity prioritize ethical conduct over short-term gains, fostering trust and credibility in their interactions with stakeholders.

Integrity in wealth accumulation extends beyond financial transactions to encompass integrity of character. Upholding principles of honesty, fairness, and accountability not only enhances one's reputation but also cultivates a culture of integrity within organizations and communities. Ultimately, integrity builds a solid foundation for sustainable wealth creation, rooted in ethical practices and responsible stewardship.

2. Transparency in Wealth Accumulation:

Transparency is essential for fostering trust and accountability in wealth accumulation. It involves openness, clarity, and disclosure of relevant information to stakeholders, including investors, employees, customers, and the public. Transparent practices enable stakeholders to make informed decisions, mitigate risks, and hold individuals and organizations accountable for their actions.

In wealth accumulation, transparency manifests in various forms, such as financial reporting, corporate governance, and communication practices. Companies that prioritize transparency demonstrate a commitment to ethical conduct and accountability, thereby enhancing investor confidence and reputation. Moreover, transparency promotes fairness and equity by ensuring equal access to information and opportunities for all stakeholders.

3. Social Responsibility in Wealth Accumulation:

Social responsibility encompasses the ethical obligations that individuals and organizations have towards society, beyond profit maximization. In the context of wealth accumulation, it involves integrating environmental, social, and governance (ESG) considerations into business practices and investment decisions. Socially responsible wealth accumulation seeks to create value not only for shareholders but also for communities, employees, and the planet.

Companies committed to social responsibility prioritize initiatives that promote environmental sustainability, social equity, and community development. This may include implementing fair labor practices, reducing carbon emissions, supporting charitable causes, and fostering diversity and inclusion. By aligning wealth accumulation with social responsibility, individuals and organizations contribute to positive social impact and long-term sustainability.

Conclusion:

Integrity, transparency, and social responsibility are essential pillars of ethical wealth accumulation. By upholding these principles, individuals and organizations not only enhance their credibility and reputation but also contribute to the greater good of society. In an increasingly interconnected and interdependent world, prioritizing integrity, transparency, and social responsibility in wealth accumulation is not only morally imperative but also essential for building a more equitable and sustainable future.

Section 3: Examination of ethical dilemmas faced by entrepreneurs, investors, and professionals in the financial industry

The financial industry is rife with ethical dilemmas that entrepreneurs, investors, and professionals grapple with on a daily basis. In this section, we explore some of the most prevalent ethical challenges faced by individuals in these roles and discuss the implications of these dilemmas on both personal and professional conduct.

1. Ethical Dilemmas for Entrepreneurs:

Entrepreneurs encounter a myriad of ethical dilemmas as they navigate the complexities of starting and scaling a business. One common dilemma is balancing the pursuit of profit with social and environmental responsibility. Entrepreneurs may face pressure to prioritize financial gain over ethical considerations, leading to decisions that compromise values or harm stakeholders.

Another ethical dilemma for entrepreneurs involves honesty and transparency in business dealings. Temptations to misrepresent products or services, inflate financial projections, or conceal information from investors can arise, particularly in competitive markets. Upholding integrity and transparency amidst such pressures requires courage and a steadfast commitment to ethical principles.

Furthermore, entrepreneurs often grapple with dilemmas related to employee treatment and workplace culture. Issues such as fair compensation, diversity and inclusion, and work-life balance can test an entrepreneur's commitment to ethical leadership and responsible management practices.

2. Ethical Dilemmas for Investors:

Investors face their own set of ethical dilemmas as they allocate capital and make investment decisions. One prominent dilemma is the tension between financial returns and ethical considerations. Investors may encounter opportunities that promise high profits but involve industries or practices that conflict with their values, such as fossil fuels, tobacco, or weapons manufacturing.

Moreover, investors must navigate the ethical implications of engaging with companies with questionable corporate governance practices or histories of ethical misconduct. Deciding whether to invest in such companies requires careful consideration of the potential risks and rewards, as well as the investor's own ethical standards.

Additionally, investors face dilemmas related to information asymmetry and insider trading. The temptation to act on nonpublic information or manipulate markets for personal gain can lead to ethical breaches and legal consequences. Upholding integrity and adhering to regulatory standards are essential for maintaining trust and credibility in the investment community.

3. Ethical Dilemmas for Professionals in the Financial Industry:

Professionals in the financial industry, including bankers, traders, and financial advisors, confront a range of ethical dilemmas in their day-to-day work. One pervasive dilemma is the conflict of interest between serving clients' best interests and maximizing personal or organizational profits. Financial professionals may face pressure to recommend products or strategies that generate fees or commissions, even if they are not in the client's best interest.

Moreover, professionals in the financial industry must navigate ethical dilemmas related to risk management and compliance. Balancing the pursuit of returns with prudent risk management practices requires making tough decisions that prioritize long-term stability and sustainability over short-term gains.

Additionally, financial professionals must uphold ethical standards in their interactions with colleagues, clients, and regulators. Issues such as confidentiality, honesty, and professional integrity are paramount in maintaining trust and credibility within the industry.

Conclusion:

Ethical dilemmas are inherent in the entrepreneurial journey, investment decision-making, and professional conduct within the financial industry. Successfully navigating these dilemmas requires a strong ethical compass, critical thinking skills, and a commitment to integrity, transparency, and social responsibility. By confronting ethical challenges with courage and moral clarity, entrepreneurs, investors, and professionals can uphold ethical standards and contribute to a more trustworthy and sustainable financial ecosystem.

Section 4: Strategies for aligning financial goals with ethical values and making socially responsible investment choices

Aligning financial goals with ethical values and making socially responsible investment choices is essential for individuals and organizations seeking to create wealth while making a positive impact on society and the environment. In this section, we explore various strategies to achieve this alignment and navigate the complexities of ethical investing.

1. Define Your Values and Priorities:

The first step in aligning financial goals with ethical values is to clarify your personal or organizational values and priorities. Reflect on the issues that matter most to you, whether it's environmental sustainability, social justice, corporate governance, or community development. By identifying your values, you can establish a framework for making ethical decisions and evaluating investment opportunities.

2. Conduct Thorough Research:

Ethical investing requires diligent research to assess the environmental, social, and governance (ESG) performance of companies and investment funds. Look beyond financial metrics to evaluate factors such as carbon footprint, labor practices, diversity and inclusion policies, and ethical leadership. Utilize resources such as ESG ratings, sustainability reports, and third-party research to inform your investment decisions.

3. Consider Impact Investing:

Impact investing involves allocating capital to companies, organizations, or projects with the intention of generating positive social or environmental impact alongside financial returns. Impact investors seek to address pressing global challenges, such as climate change, poverty alleviation, and access to healthcare and education. Explore opportunities in sectors such as renewable energy, affordable housing, sustainable agriculture, and social enterprises that align with your values and objectives.

4. Engage with Companies and Fund Managers:

Active engagement with companies and fund managers can be a powerful strategy for influencing corporate behavior and promoting positive change. Shareholder activism, proxy voting, and direct dialogue with company management can encourage greater transparency, accountability, and responsiveness to ESG issues. Collaborate with like-minded investors and advocacy groups to amplify your impact and advocate for sustainable business practices.

5. Diversify Your Portfolio:

Diversification is key to managing risk and maximizing returns in ethical investing. Build a diversified portfolio that includes a range of asset classes, sectors, and geographic regions aligned with your values and financial goals. Consider incorporating both traditional and impact investment vehicles, such as mutual funds, exchange-traded funds (ETFs), community development finance institutions (CDFIs), and green bonds, to achieve a balanced and resilient portfolio.

6. Monitor and Evaluate Performance:

Regular monitoring and evaluation of your investment portfolio are essential to track progress towards your financial and ethical objectives. Assess the impact of your investments on ESG criteria, financial returns, and broader societal outcomes. Stay informed about evolving trends, regulations, and best practices in ethical investing, and be prepared to adjust your investment strategy as needed to stay aligned with your values and goals.

Conclusion:

Aligning financial goals with ethical values and making

socially responsible investment choices requires intentionality, diligence, and ongoing commitment. By defining your values, conducting thorough research, considering impact investing opportunities, engaging with companies and fund managers, diversifying your portfolio, and monitoring performance, you can build a portfolio that not only delivers financial returns but also contributes to positive social and environmental change. By harnessing the power of finance for good, individuals and organizations can create a more sustainable and equitable future for generations to come.

CHAPTER 10: "LEGACY BUILDING: LEAVING A LASTING IMPACT BEYOND WEALTH"

Section 1: Discussion on the Concept of Legacy and Its Importance in Wealth Planning and Management

Introduction to Legacy: Legacy is a multifaceted concept that extends beyond mere financial assets. It encompasses the values, beliefs, accomplishments, and contributions an individual leaves behind for future generations. While wealth often plays a significant role in shaping legacies, true legacy-building involves more than just monetary considerations. It involves the intentional cultivation of a lasting impact on society, family, and communities.

Understanding the Importance of Legacy in Wealth Planning and Management:

Defining Values and Objectives:
Legacy planning starts with introspection and reflection on personal values, aspirations, and goals. It involves clarifying what matters most to an individual or family beyond financial success.
By defining these values and objectives, individuals can align

their wealth management strategies with their broader legacy aspirations. This ensures that financial decisions are purposeful and meaningful.

Fostering Intergenerational Wealth Transfer:
Legacy planning involves preparing the next generation to steward wealth responsibly. It goes beyond transferring financial assets to imparting values, financial literacy, and a sense of social responsibility.

Effective wealth transfer strategies include education, mentorship, and communication to ensure that heirs understand the significance of the legacy they inherit and are equipped to manage it effectively.

Impactful Philanthropy and Social Responsibility:
Philanthropy is a cornerstone of legacy-building, allowing individuals to make a positive impact on causes and issues they care about.

Wealth planning and management should incorporate philanthropic goals, whether through charitable giving, establishing foundations, or supporting social enterprises. By integrating philanthropy into their legacy, individuals can create lasting change and leave a mark on society.

Preserving Family Harmony and Values:
Family dynamics and relationships are integral to legacy planning. Wealth can either unite or divide families, depending on how it is managed and distributed.

Legacy planning involves fostering open communication, resolving conflicts, and promoting shared values within the family. This ensures that wealth serves as a unifying force rather than a source of tension.

Creating a Lasting Impact Beyond Wealth:
Legacy extends beyond financial assets to encompass personal achievements, contributions to society, and the memories

individuals leave behind.

Wealth planning and management should focus on creating a holistic legacy that encompasses professional accomplishments, personal values, and the relationships individuals cultivate throughout their lives.

Conclusion:

Legacy planning is an essential component of wealth management, emphasizing the broader impact individuals seek to achieve beyond financial success. By defining values, fostering intergenerational wealth transfer, engaging in impactful philanthropy, preserving family harmony, and creating a lasting impact, individuals can leave behind a legacy that transcends monetary wealth and enriches the lives of future generations.

Section 2: Exploration of Different Forms of Legacy

Legacy comes in various forms, extending beyond financial assets to encompass philanthropy, mentorship, community involvement, and more. Each form offers unique opportunities for individuals to make a lasting impact on society, shape future generations, and leave behind a meaningful legacy.

Philanthropy:

Philanthropy involves the strategic deployment of resources, including financial assets, time, and expertise, to address social issues and create positive change.

Individuals can establish foundations, endowments, or donor-advised funds to support causes aligned with their values and priorities.

Effective philanthropy involves thoughtful research, strategic planning, and ongoing evaluation to maximize impact and ensure resources are directed where they are most needed.

Mentorship:

Mentorship is a powerful form of legacy-building that involves sharing knowledge, experience, and guidance with others to help them achieve their goals and fulfill their potential.

Mentors play a vital role in shaping the personal and professional development of their mentees, providing support, encouragement, and valuable insights.

By serving as mentors, individuals can leave a legacy of leadership, empowerment, and knowledge transfer, nurturing the next generation of leaders and innovators.

Community Involvement:

Active participation in community initiatives, organizations, and volunteer efforts is another meaningful way to leave a lasting legacy.

Community involvement allows individuals to contribute their time, skills, and resources to address local challenges, strengthen social bonds, and build a sense of belonging.

Whether through civic engagement, charitable work, or grassroots advocacy, individuals can leave a tangible mark on their communities and inspire others to get involved.

Environmental Stewardship:

Environmental conservation and sustainability are increasingly important aspects of legacy-building, given the global challenges posed by climate change and ecological degradation.

Individuals can support conservation efforts, promote sustainable practices, and advocate for policies that protect natural resources and biodiversity.

By prioritizing environmental stewardship, individuals can leave a legacy of environmental awareness, preservation, and responsibility for future generations.

Cultural and Artistic Contributions:

Cultural and artistic pursuits offer avenues for individuals to express their creativity, preserve cultural heritage, and inspire others through their artistic endeavors.

Whether through patronage of the arts, artistic expression, or cultural preservation efforts, individuals can leave a rich cultural egacy that transcends generations.

Supporting cultural institutions, promoting artistic education, and fostering creativity within communities contribute to a vibrant cultural legacy that enriches society.

Conclusion:

Exploring different forms of legacy, including philanthropy, mentorship, community involvement, environmental stewardship, and cultural contributions, provides individuals with diverse opportunities to make a meaningful impact on society and shape the future for generations to come. By embracing these forms of legacy-building, individuals can leave behind a multifaceted legacy that reflects their values, passions, and aspirations, leaving a lasting imprint on the world.

Section 3: Practical Guidance on Creating and Executing a Legacy Plan

Creating and executing a legacy plan involves deliberate intentionality, thoughtful consideration of values, and strategic planning to ensure a lasting impact on future generations. This section provides practical guidance on crafting and implementing a comprehensive legacy plan, including strategies for passing down values, knowledge, and assets.

Clarify Your Values and Objectives:

Begin by reflecting on your core values, beliefs, and aspirations. Identify what matters most to you and what legacy you want to leave behind.

Consider the principles and lessons you wish to impart to future generations, as well as the causes or issues you are passionate about supporting.

Document Your Legacy Vision:

Write down your legacy vision, detailing the values, principles, and goals you want to instill in your heirs and contribute to society.

Articulate how you want to be remembered and the impact you hope to have on future generations, whether through philanthropy, mentorship, community involvement, or other means.

Develop a Comprehensive Estate Plan:

Work with estate planning professionals, such as lawyers, financial advisors, and accountants, to develop a comprehensive estate plan that aligns with your legacy vision.

Ensure that your estate plan addresses the transfer of financial assets, including wills, trusts, and beneficiary designations, in accordance with your wishes.

Integrate Philanthropy into Your Legacy Plan:

Incorporate philanthropic goals into your legacy plan by establishing charitable trusts, foundations, or donor-advised funds to support causes you care about.

Engage family members in philanthropic activities, fostering a spirit of giving and social responsibility across generations.

Pass Down Values and Wisdom:

Identify opportunities to pass down your values, wisdom, and life lessons to future generations through storytelling, family traditions, and meaningful conversations.

Share personal anecdotes, experiences, and insights that illustrate the importance of integrity, resilience, compassion, and other values you hold dear.

Foster Intergenerational Communication and Education:

Facilitate open and honest communication within your family, creating a supportive environment for discussing financial matters, legacy planning, and personal values.

Provide financial education and mentorship to younger family members, empowering them to manage wealth responsibly and make informed decisions.

Document Your Knowledge and Experience:

Document your knowledge, skills, and experiences in written form, audio recordings, or video testimonials to preserve your legacy for future generations.

Share practical advice, career lessons, and life insights that can guide and inspire your heirs as they navigate their own paths.

Review and Update Your Legacy Plan Regularly:

Periodically review and update your legacy plan to reflect changes in your circumstances, values, and objectives.

Stay informed about evolving estate planning laws and regulations to ensure that your plan remains current and effective.

Conclusion:

Creating and executing a legacy plan requires careful consideration, strategic planning, and ongoing commitment to passing down values, knowledge, and assets to future generations. By clarifying your values, developing a comprehensive estate plan, integrating philanthropy, passing down wisdom, fostering intergenerational communication, documenting your knowledge, and regularly reviewing your plan, you can leave behind a legacy that reflects your values, enriches the lives of others, and endures for generations to come.

Section 4: Case Studies and Examples of Individuals Leaving Lasting Impact on Society Through Wealth and Actions

Examining case studies and examples of individuals who have left a lasting impact on society through their wealth and actions offers valuable insights into effective legacy-building strategies. Here are several notable examples:

1. Greta Thunberg:

Greta Thunberg is a Swedish environmental activist known for her efforts to raise awareness about climate change and advocate for urgent action to address the global crisis.

Starting with her solitary protest outside the Swedish Parliament in 2018, Thunberg sparked a global youth movement known as Fridays for Future, inspiring millions of young people to demand climate action from world leaders.

Her passionate speeches at international forums, including the United Nations Climate Action Summit, have drawn attention to the urgency of the climate crisis and the need for immediate action.

2. Ruth Bader Ginsburg:

Ruth Bader Ginsburg, often referred to as RBG, was a pioneering lawyer and Supreme Court Justice who championed gender equality and women's rights.

As an advocate and litigator, Ginsburg played a key role in advancing legal protections against gender discrimination, arguing landmark cases before the Supreme Court.

Her jurisprudence and advocacy efforts paved the way for significant advancements in gender equality, reproductive rights, and LGBTQ+ rights in the United States.

3. Michelle Obama:

Michelle Obama, the former First Lady of the United States, has been an influential advocate for education, health, and empowerment, particularly for women and girls.

Through initiatives like Let Girls Learn and the Reach Higher campaign, Obama has promoted educational opportunities and encouraged young people to pursue their dreams.

Her memoir, "Becoming," and public appearances have inspired millions with her message of resilience, authenticity, and hope.

4. Jeff Bezos:

Jeff Bezos is the founder and former CEO of Amazon, the e-commerce giant that revolutionized online shopping and transformed the retail industry.

Under Bezos' leadership, Amazon expanded into diverse sectors, including cloud computing, artificial intelligence, and entertainment.

Bezos' entrepreneurial vision and relentless pursuit of innovation have reshaped consumer behavior and disrupted traditional business models.

5. LeBron James:

LeBron James is a professional basketball player known for his excellence on the court and his commitment to social activism and philanthropy off the court.

Through his LeBron James Family Foundation, James has invested in education initiatives, including the I PROMISE School in his hometown of Akron, Ohio, which provides comprehensive support to at-risk students.

James has used his platform to speak out on issues such as racial injustice, systemic inequality, and voting rights, leveraging his influence to effect positive change in his community and beyond.

6. Mother Teresa:

Mother Teresa, also known as Saint Teresa of Calcutta, dedicated her life to serving the poorest of the poor in Kolkata, India, and around the world.

Through her organization, the Missionaries of Charity, Mother Teresa provided food, shelter, medical care, and compassion to those in need, regardless of their religion or background.

Her selfless devotion to helping the marginalized and vulnerable inspired millions and earned her international recognition, including the Nobel Peace Prize in 1979.

7. Steve Jobs:

Jobs, the co-founder of Apple Inc., revolutionized the technology industry with innovations such as the iPhone, iPad, and Macintosh computer.

His vision for user-friendly, beautifully designed products

transformed the way people interact with technology and reshaped entire industries.

Jobs' legacy extends beyond technological innovation; his entrepreneurial spirit and commitment to excellence continue to inspire creativity and disruption in the business world.

8. Albert Einstein:

Einstein, one of the most influential scientists of the 20th century, revolutionized our understanding of the universe with his theories of relativity.

Beyond his groundbreaking contributions to physics, Einstein was a vocal advocate for pacifism, civil rights, and humanitarian causes.

His legacy of intellectual curiosity, humanitarianism, and advocacy for peace continues to inspire scientists, activists, and thinkers worldwide.

9. Wangari Maathai:

Maathai, an environmentalist and political activist from Kenya, founded the Green Belt Movement, which focused on tree planting, environmental conservation, and women's empowerment.

Through grassroots efforts, Maathai mobilized communities to plant millions of trees, combat deforestation, and promote sustainable development.

Her dedication to environmental conservation, democracy, and women's rights earned her the Nobel Peace Prize in 2004, making her the first African woman to receive the award.

10. Mahatma Gandhi:

Gandhi, the leader of India's nonviolent independence movement, inspired millions with his philosophy of satyagraha (truth-force) and ahimsa (nonviolence).

Through civil disobedience and peaceful protest, Gandhi led India to independence from British rule, demonstrating the power of moral courage and collective action.

His teachings on nonviolent resistance and social justice continue to influence movements for civil rights, freedom, and equality worldwide.

11. Marie Curie:

Marie Curie was a pioneering physicist and chemist known for her groundbreaking research on radioactivity.

As the first woman to win a Nobel Prize and the only person to win Nobel Prizes in two different scientific fields (Physics and Chemistry), Curie's work laid the foundation for advancements in nuclear physics and medical treatments.

Her legacy of scientific discovery and perseverance continues to inspire generations of scientists, particularly women in STEM fields.

12. Martin Luther King Jr.:

Martin Luther King Jr. was a prominent leader in the American civil rights movement, advocating for racial equality and nonviolent resistance.

Through his powerful speeches, peaceful protests, and civil disobedience, King played a central role in the Montgomery Bus Boycott, the March on Washington, and the passage of landmark civil rights legislation.

King's commitment to justice, equality, and nonviolence continues to resonate globally, inspiring movements for social change and human rights advocacy.

13. Clara Barton:

Clara Barton, known as the "Angel of the Battlefield," was a pioneering nurse and humanitarian who founded the American Red Cross.

During the Civil War, Barton provided medical care to wounded soldiers on the front lines, earning her widespread acclaim for her bravery and compassion.

Barton's advocacy for humanitarian aid and disaster relief laid the groundwork for the modern Red Cross movement, saving countless lives and providing assistance to those in need worldwide.

14. Florence Nightingale:

Florence Nightingale, known as the founder of modern nursing, revolutionized healthcare practices and hospital management.

During the Crimean War, Nightingale and her team of nurses improved sanitation, reduced mortality rates, and implemented evidence-based medical practices.

Nightingale's pioneering work in nursing education, public health advocacy, and patient care set new standards for healthcare delivery and established nursing as a respected profession.

15. Cesar Chavez:

Cesar Chavez was a labor leader and civil rights activist who co-founded the United Farm Workers (UFW) union to advocate for the rights of farmworkers.

Through nonviolent protests, strikes, and boycotts, Chavez fought for fair wages, better working conditions, and dignity for agricultural workers.

His tireless advocacy and grassroots organizing efforts led to significant improvements in labor rights and inspired solidarity among workers across the United States.

16. Nelson Mandela:

Mandela, the iconic anti-apartheid activist and former President of South Africa, dedicated his life to fighting racial injustice and promoting reconciliation.

Despite enduring 27 years of imprisonment, Mandela emerged as a symbol of resilience, forgiveness, and unity.

His leadership paved the way for the dismantling of apartheid and the establishment of a democratic South Africa, inspiring movements for social justice worldwide.

17. Henry Ford:

Ford, the founder of Ford Motor Company, revolutionized the automotive industry and transformed modern transportation.

Through innovations such as the assembly line, Ford made automobiles accessible to the masses, ushering in an era of mobility and economic prosperity.

Ford's contributions to industrialization and mass production have had a profound impact on global commerce and society's mobility.

18. Malala Yousafzai:

Yousafzai, a Pakistani education activist and Nobel laureate, has championed girls' rights to education in the face of adversity.

After surviving an assassination attempt by the Taliban for her advocacy, Yousafzai became a global symbol of courage and resilience.

Through the Malala Fund, she continues to advocate for universal access to education, empowering girls to pursue their dreams and break barriers.

19. Andrew Goodman, James Chaney, and Michael Schwerner:

Goodman, Chaney, and Schwerner were civil rights activists who were tragically murdered during the Freedom Summer of 1964 in Mississippi, USA.

Their deaths galvanized support for the civil rights movement and led to the passage of the Civil Rights Act of 1964, which outlawed segregation and discrimination.

Their sacrifice and commitment to justice remain emblematic of the ongoing struggle for racial equality and social justice.

20. J.K. Rowling:

Rowling, the author of the Harry Potter series, has captivated readers worldwide with her imaginative storytelling and themes of friendship, courage, and resilience.

Beyond literary success, Rowling has used her platform to advocate for social issues such as children's welfare, literacy, and equality.

Through initiatives like Lumos, Rowling works to end the institutionalization of children and promote family-based care around the world.

21. Fred Rogers:

Rogers, known as the creator and host of the television series "Mister Rogers' Neighborhood," dedicated his life to promoting kindness, empathy, and emotional well-being among children.

Through his gentle demeanor and heartfelt messages, Rogers became a beloved figure in children's television, teaching generations the importance of compassion and understanding.

Rogers' legacy continues to inspire acts of kindness and promote positive social interactions among people of all ages.

22. Andrew Carnegie:

Carnegie, one of the wealthiest individuals of his time, dedicated much of his fortune to philanthropy.

His contributions include funding the construction of over 2,500 libraries worldwide, establishing Carnegie Mellon University, and supporting various educational and cultural institutions.

Carnegie's philanthropic legacy continues to benefit communities and promote access to education and knowledge globally.

23. Bill and Melinda Gates:

The Gates Foundation, established by Bill and Melinda Gates, is one of the largest private philanthropic foundations in the world.

The foundation focuses on addressing global health crises, combating poverty, and improving education outcomes.

Through initiatives such as the Global Fund to Fight AIDS, Tuberculosis, and Malaria, the Gates Foundation has made significant strides in improving healthcare and reducing poverty worldwide.

24. Buffett:

Buffett, known as one of the most successful investors in history, has pledged to give away the majority of his wealth to philanthropic causes.

He has partnered with Bill and Melinda Gates to launch the Giving Pledge, encouraging other billionaires to commit to donating a significant portion of their wealth to charity.

Buffett's philanthropic efforts aim to address systemic issues such as poverty, healthcare disparities, and access to education.

25. Oprah Winfrey:

Winfrey, a media mogul and philanthropist, has leveraged her platform to promote social causes and empower individuals.

Through initiatives like the Oprah Winfrey Foundation, she has supported education, leadership development, and empowerment programs for women and girls.

Winfrey's advocacy for literacy, childhood education, and mental health awareness has had a profound impact on millions of lives.

26.Elon Musk:

Musk, the founder and CEO of SpaceX and Tesla, has focused on advancing technologies with the potential to address pressing global challenges.

His investments in sustainable energy, space exploration, and transportation innovation aim to mitigate climate change and expand humanity's reach beyond Earth.

Musk's visionary approach to entrepreneurship and commitment to ambitious goals have inspired innovation and spurred progress in multiple industries.

27. Maya Angelou:

Angelou, a renowned poet, author, and civil rights activist, left a lasting legacy through her literary works and advocacy for social justice.

Her memoir, "I Know Why the Caged Bird Sings," and poems such as "Still I Rise" continue to resonate with readers worldwide, inspiring resilience and empowerment.

Angelou's contributions to literature and civil rights activism have left an indelible mark on American culture and continue to inspire future generations.

Conclusion:

These case studies illustrate the diverse ways in which individuals can leave a lasting impact on society through their wealth and actions. Whether through philanthropy, entrepreneurship, advocacy, or artistic expression, these individuals have demonstrated the power of leveraging resources and influence to effect positive change and shape the future for generations to come. Their legacies serve as inspirations for others seeking to make a meaningful difference in the world.

CHAPTER 11: "THE PATH FORWARD: INTEGRATING WISDOM INTO ACTION"

Section 1: Recapitulation of Key Insights and Lessons Learned Throughout the Book

In this section, we embark on a comprehensive journey through the key insights and lessons learned from the preceding chapters, synthesizing the diverse perspectives and strategies discussed. The culmination of wisdom gathered from various sources and experiences provides a roadmap for integrating these insights into actionable steps for personal and collective growth.

Understanding the Nature of Wisdom:

The journey begins with an exploration of the multifaceted nature of wisdom. We have learned that wisdom encompasses more than mere knowledge; it involves a deep understanding of human nature, empathy, compassion, and the ability to navigate complex situations with discernment and humility.

Cultivating Self-Awareness:

Central to the pursuit of wisdom is the cultivation of self-awareness. Through introspection and reflection, individuals can gain insight into their values, beliefs, and motivations. Recognizing our strengths and limitations allows us to make more informed decisions and engage in authentic interactions with others.

Embracing Diversity and Perspective Taking:

We have discovered the transformative power of embracing diversity and practicing perspective-taking. By actively seeking out and listening to different viewpoints, we expand our understanding of the world and develop greater empathy towards others. Embracing diversity fosters creativity, innovation, and collaboration, enabling us to tackle complex challenges more effectively.

Navigating Uncertainty and Adversity:

Life is replete with uncertainties and adversities, yet wisdom provides a guiding light in times of darkness. Through resilience and adaptability, individuals can navigate uncertainty with courage and grace. Embracing challenges as opportunities for growth fosters resilience and empowers us to thrive amidst adversity.

Fostering Meaningful Connections:

At the heart of wisdom lies the importance of fostering meaningful connections with others. Building strong relationships based on trust, respect, and mutual understanding enriches our lives and enhances our well-being. Cultivating empathy and compassion strengthens social bonds and fosters a sense of belonging and community.

Practicing Gratitude and Mindfulness:

Gratitude and mindfulness serve as potent tools for cultivating wisdom and enhancing life satisfaction. By cultivating a mindset of gratitude, individuals can appreciate the abundance in their lives and find joy in the present moment. Mindfulness practices, such as meditation and deep breathing, help cultivate presence and awareness, fostering inner peace and clarity of mind.

Embracing Lifelong Learning:
The pursuit of wisdom is a lifelong journey characterized by curiosity and a thirst for knowledge. Embracing a growth mindset and a willingness to learn from both successes and failures fuels personal and professional development. Lifelong learning empowers individuals to adapt to change, expand their horizons, and unlock their full potential.

Taking Action with Intention and Integrity:
Ultimately, wisdom is not merely a theoretical concept but a call to action. Integrating wisdom into our daily lives requires deliberate intention and steadfast commitment. By aligning our actions with our values and principles, we can make a positive impact on the world and leave a meaningful legacy for future generations.

In conclusion, the journey towards wisdom is an ongoing process of self-discovery, growth, and transformation. By embracing the key insights and lessons learned throughout this book, we can embark on a path of personal and collective evolution, enriching our lives and the lives of those around us. As we navigate the complexities of the modern world, let us strive to cultivate wisdom in thought, word, and deed, paving the way for a brighter and more enlightened future.

Section 2: Reflection on the Transformative Journey of Self-Discovery and Empowerment

In this section, we delve into the transformative journey of self-discovery and empowerment embarked upon by the reader throughout their engagement with the book. This journey is characterized by profound introspection, growth, and the cultivation of inner strength and resilience.

Initiating the Journey:

The reader embarks on this journey of self-discovery with a sense of curiosity and openness to new perspectives. As they delve into the pages of the book, they are met with insights and wisdom that challenge their existing beliefs and assumptions, igniting a spark of curiosity and self-reflection.

Exploring Inner Landscapes:

Through introspective exercises and reflective prompts, the reader delves into the depths of their inner landscapes, uncovering hidden truths, desires, and fears. They confront aspects of themselves that have long been neglected or overlooked, gaining a deeper understanding of their values, passions, and aspirations.

Confronting Limiting Beliefs and Fears:

Along the journey, the reader confronts limiting beliefs and fears that have held them back from realizing their full potential. With courage and vulnerability, they challenge these internal barriers, embracing a mindset of growth and possibility. They recognize that true empowerment lies in transcending self-imposed limitations and embracing the inherent resilience within.

Cultivating Self-Compassion and Acceptance:

Central to the journey of self-discovery is the cultivation of self-compassion and acceptance. The reader learns to treat themselves with kindness and understanding, embracing their flaws and imperfections as integral parts of their unique journey. Through self-compassion, they find the strength to navigate challenges with grace and resilience.

Embracing Authenticity and Vulnerability:

As the reader delves deeper into their journey, they embrace authenticity and vulnerability as pathways to personal growth and connection. They let go of the need to present a façade of perfection and instead embrace their true selves, flaws and all. By embracing vulnerability, they forge deeper connections with others and cultivate a greater sense of belonging and authenticity.

Celebrating Personal Growth and Milestones:
Along the journey, the reader celebrates moments of personal growth and milestones, no matter how small. They acknowledge the progress they have made and the lessons they have learned, cultivating a sense of gratitude and appreciation for their journey. Each step forward becomes a testament to their resilience and determination.

Forging a Path of Empowerment:
Empowered by their newfound self-awareness and inner strength, the reader forges a path of empowerment in their personal and professional lives. They make bold decisions aligned with their values and passions, unafraid to take risks and pursue their dreams. Through their actions, they inspire others to embark on their own journeys of self-discovery and empowerment.

Continuing the Journey:
The journey of self-discovery and empowerment is ongoing, marked by moments of triumph and challenge. The reader recognizes that true wisdom lies in embracing the journey itself, with all its twists and turns. Armed with newfound insights and resilience, they continue to navigate the complexities of life with courage, grace, and authenticity.

In conclusion, the transformative journey of self-discovery and empowerment embarked upon by the reader is a testament to the resilience of the human spirit and the power of introspection and growth. By embracing vulnerability, cultivating self-compassion, and aligning their actions with their values, the reader charts a course towards a more fulfilling and authentic life. As they continue on their journey, they inspire others to embark on their own path of self-discovery and empowerment, creating a ripple effect of positive change in the world.

Section 3: Empowerment of Readers to Take Actionable Steps Towards Their Financial Goals

In this section, we delve into empowering readers to take actionable steps towards their financial goals, integrating newfound wisdom and mindset shifts acquired throughout their journey of self-discovery and empowerment.

Cultivating Financial Literacy:

The journey towards financial empowerment begins with cultivating financial literacy. Readers are encouraged to deepen their understanding of key financial concepts such as budgeting, saving, investing, and debt management. Through education and awareness, they gain the knowledge and confidence to make informed decisions about their finances.

Setting Clear and Achievable Goals:

With newfound clarity and self-awareness, readers are empowered to set clear and achievable financial goals. By defining their priorities and aspirations, they create a roadmap for success and stay focused on what truly matters to them. Setting SMART (Specific, Measurable, Achievable, Relevant, Time-bound) goals helps readers stay motivated and accountable.

Embracing a Growth Mindset:

A fundamental aspect of financial empowerment is embracing a growth mindset towards money. Readers learn to view setbacks and challenges as opportunities for growth and learning, rather than insurmountable obstacles. By adopting a positive and resilient attitude, they cultivate the belief that they have the power to shape their financial destiny.

Practicing Mindful Spending and Saving:

Mindful spending and saving practices are integral to achieving financial wellness. Readers are encouraged to examine their spending habits and identify areas where they can make conscious choices to align their spending with their values and goals. By prioritizing needs over wants and practicing delayed gratification, they cultivate financial discipline and resilience.

Building a Diversified Income Portfolio:

In today's rapidly changing economy, building a diversified income portfolio is essential for long-term financial security. Readers are empowered to explore diverse income streams such as entrepreneurship, freelancing, passive income investments, and side hustles. By diversifying their income sources, they mitigate risk and create multiple pathways to financial success.

Investing in Personal and Professional Development:

Investing in personal and professional development is a powerful way to enhance earning potential and career advancement. Readers are encouraged to seek opportunities for continuous learning, skill-building, and networking. By investing in themselves, they expand their knowledge base, increase their earning capacity, and unlock new opportunities for financial growth.

Managing Debt Wisely:

Debt management is a crucial aspect of financial empowerment. Readers are empowered to develop a strategic plan for paying off debt, prioritizing high-interest debt and adopting a proactive approach to repayment. By reducing debt burden and freeing up financial resources, they gain greater flexibility and autonomy in pursuing their goals.

Seeking Professional Guidance and Support:

Recognizing the value of expert advice, readers are encouraged to seek professional guidance and support from financial advisors, mentors, and coaches. By leveraging the expertise of trusted professionals, they gain personalized insights and strategies tailored to their unique financial situation and goals.

Building a Legacy of Generosity and Impact:
True financial empowerment goes beyond personal gain; it involves using wealth as a tool for positive change and impact. Readers are encouraged to embrace a mindset of abundance and generosity, incorporating philanthropy and social responsibility into their financial plans. By giving back to their communities and supporting causes they believe in, they create a legacy of generosity and impact that extends far beyond their own lifetime.

In conclusion, the empowerment of readers to take actionable steps towards their financial goals is a transformative journey that integrates newfound wisdom, mindset shifts, and practical strategies for financial success. By cultivating financial literacy, setting clear goals, embracing a growth mindset, and investing in personal development, readers can take control of their financial future and create a life of abundance, fulfillment, and impact. As they embark on this journey, they inspire others to do the same, creating a ripple effect of empowerment and prosperity in their communities and beyond.

Section4: Encouragement to Embrace Lifelong Learning and Adaptability

In this section, we explore the importance of embracing lifelong learning and adaptability as essential tools for navigating the ever-changing landscape of wealth creation. As the world evolves at a rapid pace, individuals who prioritize continuous learning and adaptability are better equipped to thrive amidst uncertainty and complexity.

The Imperative of Lifelong Learning:
Lifelong learning is the cornerstone of personal and professional development in the 21st century. Readers are

encouraged to cultivate a mindset of curiosity and a thirst for knowledge, embracing learning as a lifelong journey rather than a destination. By staying curious and open-minded, they remain agile and adaptable in the face of new challenges and opportunities.

Expanding Horizons Through Education:
Education serves as a powerful catalyst for wealth creation and personal growth. Readers are encouraged to invest in formal and informal educational opportunities, whether through traditional academic pathways, online courses, workshops, or mentorship programs. By expanding their knowledge base and skillset, they unlock new pathways to success and prosperity.

Embracing Innovation and Creativity:
In today's rapidly changing economy, innovation and creativity are key drivers of wealth creation. Readers are encouraged to embrace a spirit of innovation, seeking out new ideas, technologies, and business models that disrupt traditional paradigms. By fostering a culture of innovation and experimentation, they position themselves at the forefront of emerging trends and opportunities.

Adapting to Technological Advancements:
Technological advancements are reshaping the landscape of wealth creation, presenting both challenges and opportunities. Readers are encouraged to embrace emerging technologies such as artificial intelligence, blockchain, and digital platforms, leveraging them to streamline processes, enhance productivity, and create new sources of value. By staying abreast of technological trends and advancements, they remain competitive in an increasingly digital world.

Navigating Economic and Market Shifts:
Economic and market shifts are inevitable in a dynamic global economy. Readers are encouraged to cultivate a deep

understanding of macroeconomic trends, market dynamics, and geopolitical developments, enabling them to anticipate and adapt to changing conditions. By diversifying their investment portfolios, hedging against risks, and staying agile in their decision-making, they mitigate downside risks and capitalize on emerging opportunities.

Resilience in the Face of Adversity:

Resilience is a core attribute of individuals who navigate the ever-changing landscape of wealth creation with success. Readers are encouraged to cultivate resilience by embracing failure as a learning opportunity, bouncing back from setbacks with determination and grit, and maintaining a positive outlook in the face of adversity. By reframing challenges as opportunities for growth and learning, they emerge stronger and more resilient in the pursuit of their goals.

Building a Network of Support and Collaboration:

Collaboration and networking play a crucial role in wealth creation and adaptation. Readers are encouraged to build a diverse network of mentors, advisors, peers, and collaborators who can provide guidance, support, and opportunities for growth. By leveraging the collective wisdom and resources of their network, they amplify their impact and create synergies that propel them towards their goals.

Embracing Change as a Catalyst for Growth:

Change is inevitable in life and business, and those who embrace it with agility and adaptability are better positioned for success. Readers are encouraged to embrace change as a catalyst for growth and innovation, rather than resisting or fearing it. By remaining flexible and adaptable in their mindset and approach, they navigate uncertainty with confidence and resilience.

In conclusion, the encouragement to embrace lifelong learning and adaptability as essential tools for navigating the ever-changing landscape of wealth creation is a call to action for readers to cultivate a growth mindset, stay agile in their approach, and remain resilient in the face of adversity. By prioritizing continuous learning, embracing innovation, and adapting to change, they unlock new opportunities for prosperity and fulfillment in an increasingly dynamic world. As they embark on this journey of growth and adaptation, they inspire others to do the same, creating a ripple effect of positive change and innovation in their communities and beyond.

Section 5: Inspiration to Cultivate a Mindset of Abundance, Resilience, and Purpose

In this section, we delve into the importance of cultivating a mindset of abundance, resilience, and purpose, empowering readers to transcend societal expectations and pursue their unique path to success. By embracing these core principles, readers can unlock their full potential and create a life of fulfillment, impact, and meaning.

Embracing an Abundance Mindset:
An abundance mindset is grounded in the belief that opportunities are limitless and that success is not a zero-sum game. Readers are encouraged to shift their perspective from scarcity to abundance, recognizing that there is enough wealth, resources, and opportunities to go around. By adopting an abundance mindset, they cultivate optimism, creativity, and a sense of possibility, empowering them to pursue their goals with confidence and enthusiasm.

Cultivating Resilience in the Face of Adversity:
Resilience is a key trait of individuals who thrive in the face of challenges and setbacks. Readers are inspired to cultivate resilience by developing coping mechanisms, building a strong support network, and reframing adversity as an opportunity for growth. By embracing resilience, they bounce back from setbacks

with greater strength and determination, turning obstacles into stepping stones towards success.

Clarifying Personal Values and Purpose:
Central to the pursuit of success and fulfillment is clarifying one's personal values and purpose. Readers are encouraged to reflect on what truly matters to them, identifying their core values, passions, and aspirations. By aligning their goals and actions with their values and purpose, they create a sense of meaning and direction that guides their journey towards success.

Breaking Free from Societal Expectations:
Society often imposes rigid expectations and norms that dictate what success should look like. Readers are inspired to break free from these societal expectations and define success on their own terms. By embracing their unique strengths, talents, and passions, they create a vision of success that is authentic and fulfilling to them, regardless of external validation or approval.

Embracing Risk and Embracing Failure:
Success often requires taking calculated risks and embracing the possibility of failure. Readers are encouraged to step outside their comfort zones, embrace uncertainty, and take bold actions towards their goals. By reframing failure as a natural part of the learning process, they cultivate a growth mindset and resilience in the face of setbacks. Each failure becomes a valuable lesson that propels them closer to success.

Fostering a Culture of Gratitude and Generosity:
Gratitude and generosity are powerful antidotes to feelings of scarcity and fear. Readers are inspired to cultivate a culture of gratitude by counting their blessings, expressing appreciation for the abundance in their lives, and giving back to others. By fostering a spirit of generosity, they create a virtuous cycle of abundance that enriches their lives and those around them.

Pursuing Impact and Contribution:

True success is not measured solely by material wealth or status but by the impact we make on the world and the lives of others. Readers are encouraged to pursue success with a sense of purpose and contribution, seeking to make a meaningful difference in the lives of others. By aligning their goals with a higher purpose and focusing on service and impact, they create a legacy that extends far beyond themselves.

Celebrating Progress and Milestones:

Along the journey towards success and fulfillment, it's important to celebrate progress and milestones, no matter how small. Readers are encouraged to acknowledge their achievements, express gratitude for their growth, and celebrate the journey itself. By celebrating progress, they reinforce positive habits and mindset shifts, fueling their motivation and momentum towards greater success.

In conclusion, the inspiration to cultivate a mindset of abundance, resilience, and purpose empowers readers to transcend societal expectations and pursue their unique path to success. By embracing these core principles, they unlock their full potential, create a life of fulfillment and impact, and inspire others to do the same. As they embark on this journey of self-discovery and empowerment, they become agents of positive change, creating a ripple effect of abundance, resilience, and purpose in their communities and beyond.

Section 6: Invitation to Join a Community of Like-Minded Individuals

In this section, readers are invited to join a vibrant community of like-minded individuals who are committed to supporting each other on their journey towards financial freedom and fulfillment. This community serves as a source of inspiration, encouragement, and practical support, empowering members to overcome challenges, celebrate successes, and grow together.

Creating a Supportive Network:
The community provides a supportive environment where members can connect with others who share similar goals, values, and aspirations. By fostering meaningful relationships and mutual support, members feel empowered to overcome obstacles and pursue their dreams with confidence.

Sharing Knowledge and Resources:
Within the community, members have the opportunity to share valuable knowledge, insights, and resources related to personal finance, wealth creation, and personal development. Through collaborative learning and knowledge exchange, members gain access to diverse perspectives and practical strategies for achieving their financial goals.

Accountability and Motivation:
Accountability is a key driver of success in any endeavor. By participating in the community, members commit to holding themselves and each other accountable for taking action towards their financial goals. Regular check-ins, goal-setting exercises, and progress updates provide members with the motivation and encouragement they need to stay focused and disciplined.
Celebrating Successes and Milestones:
The community serves as a platform for celebrating successes, big and small. Members have the opportunity to share their achievements, milestones, and breakthroughs, inspiring others and reinforcing a culture of positivity and achievement. By celebrating each other's successes, members feel valued, supported, and encouraged to continue on their journey towards financial freedom and fulfillment.

Offering Emotional Support and Encouragement:
Navigating the ups and downs of the financial journey can be emotionally challenging. In the community, members find a

safe space to share their struggles, fears, and setbacks without judgment. Empathetic listening, compassionate support, and words of encouragement from fellow members help lift spirits, build resilience, and foster a sense of belonging and camaraderie.

Collaboration and Partnership Opportunities:
The community serves as a platform for collaboration and partnership opportunities, enabling members to leverage each other's skills, expertise, and resources for mutual benefit. Whether through joint ventures, business partnerships, or collaborative projects, members have the chance to amplify their impact and achieve greater success together than they could alone.

Giving Back and Paying It Forward:
As members achieve success and reach their financial goals, they are encouraged to give back to the community and pay it forward. Whether through mentorship, volunteering, or charitable giving, members have the opportunity to make a positive impact in the lives of others and contribute to the greater good. By giving back, they reinforce a culture of generosity, abundance, and collective empowerment within the community.

In conclusion, the invitation to join a community of like-minded individuals committed to supporting each other on their journey towards financial freedom and fulfillment is an opportunity for readers to connect with a supportive network of peers, gain valuable knowledge and resources, and receive the encouragement and accountability they need to achieve their goals. By joining forces with others who share similar values and aspirations, readers can accelerate their progress, overcome challenges, and create a life of abundance, resilience, and purpose.

UTILIZING ARTIFICIAL INTELLIGENCE FOR PERSONALIZED MANAGEMENT OF PREGNANCY SICKNESS:
CHALLENGES, OPPORTUNITIES, AND FUTURE DIRECTIONS

BY

HENRY E. PARKINS

COPYRIGHT PAGE